Introduction

Twenty-first century students work to improve their ability to proficiently and independently read a wide range of complex texts from various content areas. *Lincoln Empowered Text Collection* is a compilation of literature that provides informational texts, essays, newspaper articles, fables, legends, poetry, short stories, plays, persuasive letters, business letters, diary and journal entries, and more to students learning to read and students reading to learn alike. Even at a young age, students who engage in the careful, meaningful reading of a variety of works develop their ability to:

- Evaluate texts for story elements, literary devices, and/or text features.
- Construct effective arguments based on the content read.
- Discern authors' points of view.
- Ask questions.
- Build vocabulary.
- Gain general and content-specific knowledge.
- Build a stronger worldview through exposure to cultural and era-specific pieces.

This book's contents include all literary pieces used in Empowered courses for one grade level. For easy access, the texts are given in the order in which they appear in Empowered courses.

This collection aligns with the most recent course content at the time of printing.

Contents

Dinosaur Day 1
written by Sarah Marino

The Mangled Mirror Tragedy 5
written by Jennifer Tkocs

Ingroy and the Walrus of Udlam:
Introductions 1, 2, and 3 7
written by Summer York

Stella's Missing Bear 8
written by Jennifer Tkocs

Rising Action in Bunnicula............................ 10
written by Summer York

Jay and the Race.. 11
written by Sarah Marino

Story Climax in Mulan 15
written by Summer York

The Old Rabbit and the Sly Fox: An Aesop's Fable.... 16
adapted by Jill Fisher

Falling Action in Sleeping Beauty 18
written by Summer York

How Sofia Tamed the Dragon........................ 19
written by Summer York

Abstract Nouns 22
written by Mark Weimer

Postcards from Pismo: A Report 23
written by Mark Weimer

Augusta Rain: Secret Superhero 24
transcribed by Sarah Marino

The Fisherman and the Little Fish................ 28
adapted by Sarah Marino

Pandora.. 30
adapted by Sarah Marino

The Concert.. 33
written by Summer York

The High Dive.. 34
written by Summer York

Little Red Riding Hood.................................. 35
adapted by Michael Scotto

Twenty Dollars Each 37
written by Katie Catanzarite

The Three Little Pigs...................................... 38
adapted by Ashley Bell

Theme: "The Boy Who Cried Wolf" 39
written by Summer York

A Conflict at the Playground 40
written by Summer York

Theme: *Little House on the Prairie*............... 42
written by Summer York

The Librarian... 43
written by Katie Catanzarite

Gum, Now and Then 45
written by Bryon Gill

The Runt Horse.. 47
written by Sarah Marino

Popcorn Explosion Causes Kernel Chaos
in Local Neighborhood.................................. 50
written by Summer York

A Swing Set Story 53
written by Vincent J. Scotto

Joel's Birthday.. 55
written by Jennifer Tkocs

Jake and Jake 57
written by Mark Weimer

King Midas and the Golden Touch 58
written by Debbie Parrish

Book Report: *Charlie and the Chocolate Factory*....... 61
written by Luke See

Book Report: *Matilda* 62
written by Luke See

Book Report: Stuart Little 63
written by Luke See

Book Report: *The Velveteen Rabbit* 64
written by Luke See

TAM, TAM, the Answer Man.................................. 65
written by Debbie Parrish

Postcards from Pismo:
Timeline of Important Events.................................. 68
written by Summer York

The Old Man and the Magical Deer........................ 71
written by Jill Fisher

Dinner is Served 74
written by Katie Catanzarite

It's a Dog's Life 75
written by Debbie Parrish

Birthday Parties and Basketballs 77
written by Katie Catanzarite

My Annoying Best Friend.................................. 79
written by Vincent J. Scotto

The Legend of the No Face Doll 81
adapted by Debbie Parrish

The Perfect Pair.................................. 84
written by Vincent J. Scotto

Anansi and the River: An Ashanti Folktale................ 86
adapted by Vincent J. Scotto

Aunt Nancy and the Swamp:
A Southern American Folktale 88
adapted by Vincent J. Scotto

Jasmine and the Song.................................. 90
written by Jill Fisher

Choosing Bedtimes: An Opinion Article.................... 92
written by Mark Weimer

The Girl with the Golden Teeth.......................... 93
written by Katie Catanzarite

Hydraulic Fracturing 94
written by Mark Weimer

The Third Grade Gumshoe 96
written by Summer York

An Exceprt from "The Ride".......................... 98
written by Jennifer Tkocs

A Ghost in the Window.................................. 99
written by Summer York

Yogurt.................................. 101
written by Mark Weimer

Life in New York City.................................. 102
written by Jill Fisher

The Rewards of Recycling 104
written by Luke See

The History of Numbers.................................. 106
written by Megan Weinman

Amazing National Parks:
Volcanoes and Mountains 108
written by Jill Fisher

Nurturing Nature: The Life of Rachel Carson 110
written by Michael Scotto

Ruby Bridges: A Brave Girl Who
Changed History 114
written by Jennifer Tkocs

Thump in the Night.................................. 116
written by Vincent J. Scotto

Amelia Earhart.................................. 118
written by Jennifer Tkocs

A Horse and Paul Revere.................................. 120
written by Mark Weimer

Ten-Year-Old Rescues Kitten from Tree 121
written by Katie Catanzarite

The Constitution of the United States 122
written by Vincent J. Scotto

Researching Made Simple 124
written by Vincent J. Scotto

Igneous Rock (First, Second, and Third Hooks) 125
written by Vincent J. Scotto

Ford's Assembly Line 127
written by Summer York

Dialogue: The Story Enhancer 129
written by Luke See

Farm Living 130
written by Debbie Parrish

Jane Goodall 132
written by Summer York

From Seed to Fruit 134
written by Luke See

The Importance of Flossing 136
written by Mark Weimer

Put Cell Phones: Past, Present, and Future 137
written by Jill Fisher

Rain Forests: Nature's Pharmacy 139
written by Luke See

Saving the Rain Forests 140
written by Luke See

Self-Driving Cars: A Smarter Route 141
written by Vincent J. Scotto

Self-Driving Cars: A Dangerous Path 142
written by Vincent J. Scotto

How the United States Was Shaped 143
written by Jill Fisher

The Pacific Coast Gem: A Memorable
Tour by Train 145
written by Sarah Marino

The Koala 147
written by Luke See

Benefits of Children Learning a
Musical Instrument 149
written by Katie Catanzarite

George the Great and Powerful 150
written by Jennifer Tkocs

Betrayal of Mathematical Proportions 153
written by Summer York

Sunrise in the Desert 155
written by Jennifer Tkocs

A Girl's Future 156
written by Summer York

Strength 157
written by Summer York

Rain and Baseball 158
written by Steve Karscig

Climbing Magnolias 159
written by Steve Karscig

Swinging on Weeping Willows 160
written by Steve Karscig

The Great Aluminum Knight 161
written by Steve Karscig

The Vision of Gwen 165
written by Steve Karscig

Stone Soup 168
adapted by Michael Scotto

Two Scenes from *The Thief of Camelot* 187
written by Luke See

The Olympic Games: A History of Evolving
Competition 192
written by Vincent J. Scotto

Rain Barrels 194
written by Mark Weimer

Charlotte's Web: A Lesson in Friendship 195
written by Summer York

Presentation Nerves 196
written by Summer York

The Value of Timed Writing Exercises 198
written by Jennifer Tkocs

Apple 199
written by Summer York

Turning Off Niagra Falls: A News Report 200
written by Summer York

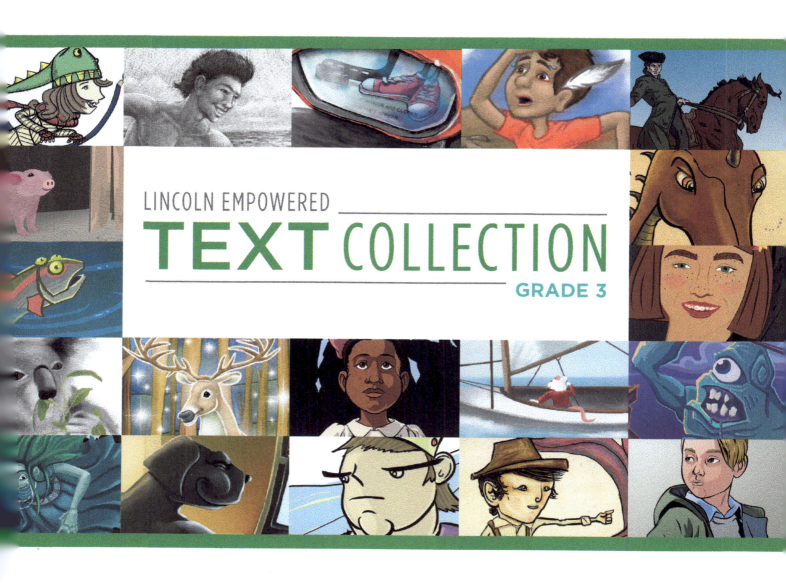

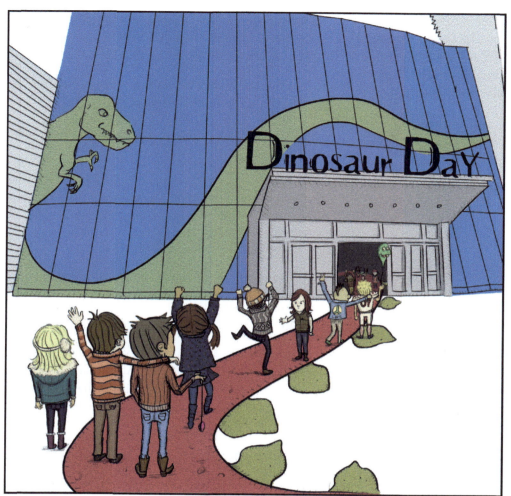

Dinosaur Day

written by Sarah Marino
illustrated by David Rushbrook

Abby and her classmates stood in a line inside the science center, in front of a window that was the size of an entire wall. It seemed like they had been waiting forever for their teachers, Mrs. Gibson and Miss Walters, to tell them what to do next.

The floor where they stood was lit up by sunlight coming in the window. Outside the window was a small garden with a fountain and statues. It was a breezy, autumn Tuesday, and dry, colorful leaves swirled around the fountain, some of them coming to rest in the murky water. In the distance, Abby could see the harbor and a few big boats sitting gently in the middle of it.

The third-grade class from Woodlawn Elementary was at the Maryland Science Center in Baltimore. They were going to see Dinosaur Mysteries. In their science lessons, they were learning all about dinosaurs. They were reading about them, watching videos, and playing games with dinosaur characters.

Abby had been looking forward to Dinosaur Day for six weeks. She had been the first to turn in a signed permission form. She did not even mind that she and her classmates would have to write the names of the dinosaurs they saw in their notebooks and do a worksheet for homework.

"I can't wait to see t. rex," Abby said to her friend Pamela, who was her field trip partner.

Pamela sighed, blinking and looking up to the ceiling before looking back at Abby. "I don't get why you're so excited, Abby. We have to do homework for this."

"So what? I like dinosaurs," Abby said, looking straight into Pamela's eyes. Abby felt only slightly surprised at Pamela's bad mood, which was not really new but was starting to show itself more often.

"Well, I've been to the science center so many times," Pamela said. "The dinosaurs aren't that great." She paused and then said, "You're starting to act like Andrew."

Abby looked around and saw Andrew. He and Daniel had found the Hall of Minerals. They were a few feet away from the class. Their noses were almost smashed against a glass case that held a sparkling, bright yellow gem. These boys were known as teachers' pets. Most kids would play ball or jump rope at recess. Andrew and Daniel would sit and read, or stare at bugs through bulky magnifying lenses.

Still, Abby didn't mind Andrew. She thought he was clever. She liked his excited way of talking about things, even if they were gross things sometimes. She wouldn't feel right trying to explain these feelings to Pamela though.

"What are they doing?" Pamela asked, looking at Andrew and Daniel. "They're going to get in trouble." She shook her head and pulled her blond braid from one shoulder to the other.

Abby was just about to point out that she and Pamela had been to the science center over the summer with Pamela's parents. Pamela had been glad to be there then; but before she could say it, Andrew came rushing toward them. He almost fell on the shiny, slippery floor.

"Abby, have you ever seen a yellow sapphire?" he asked, his eyes the size of dinosaur eggs.

"No, I haven't, Andrew," Abby said in an interested way.

"You should really come and check it out. It looks like gold if the light hits it just the right way. They are very rare. That one was found in Montana," he said.

"Wow, that's pretty cool," Abby said.

"Come on, I'll show you," he said.

"We can't leave the line, Andrew," Pamela said sharply. Her face began to turn red.

"Okay, class, listen up." They turned to see Mrs. Gibson at the front of the line. Abby really liked Mrs. Gibson, especially since Mrs. Gibson had told Abby what a great job she'd done in the science fair last week.

"Well, maybe later, Abby," Andrew said and smiled. He took his place in line beside Daniel a few feet ahead.

"Geez, Abby," Pamela said. "Maybe you should just be his partner already!"

"Well, at least he doesn't act like he doesn't like dinosaurs!" Abby said, her voice louder than she had planned. She felt like continuing the argument with Pamela, but the line started to move. Even though she was angry, she didn't want to get in trouble or ruin this day at the science center.

"Stay in line now," Miss Walters said, "and keep close to your partner. We don't want anyone getting lost."

A mean part of Abby wished that Pamela would get lost. She wished Pamela were not her partner. Abby gazed around her and saw that everyone else already had a partner. She knew she would feel bad leaving Pamela anyhow, even if her friend had decided to be a grump. She hoped Pamela would not mope for the entire walk through Dinosaur Mysteries.

To avoid seeing Pamela as they walked, Abby turned to look out the window wall. Orange and yellow leaves fluttered in the wind around the funny-looking statues. Miss Walters had said that the one that looked like a lion had been brought here all the way from London. Abby wanted to remember to tell her parents that, because they had met in London. Abby was not sure where London was exactly, but she knew it was all the way across the Atlantic Ocean, on an island.

Their line moved past the entrance to the Hall of Minerals and around a corner. They stopped in a large room before two giant doors of frosted glass.

"Class, we'll enter the dinosaur exhibit now," Miss Walters said, as she stood before the doors that led into Dinosaur Mysteries. "Please write down in your notebook the name of each dinosaur, along with two facts about each one. Feel free to sit on the floor to write in your notebook. Just be sure you're off to the side of the walking path. Any questions?"

No one had questions, so Miss Walters and Mrs. Gibson held open the doors and let the class walk in ahead of them. The homeroom parents were at the front of the line.

Inside, next to the allosaurus, was a map on a large computer screen. Mrs. Gibson explained that it showed what the earth's continents and oceans looked like during the dinosaurs' time. The land was almost all in one piece. Abby wondered where Baltimore would have been on this map.

They turned a corner and Abby almost gasped at the sight of the Tyrannosaurus rex. Even though she had been to the center several times before, the sight of him always surprised her and made her a little giggly. She almost walked straight into Emma Barton because her gaze was on the t. rex.

"Wow, that is really big," Emma said to her partner, Lindsay.

"It is!" Lindsay replied.

"T. rex had a head that was five feet long, with teeth that were six inches!" Andrew said. He and Daniel were just in front of Emma and Lindsay in the line.

"And their bodies were almost fifty feet long. My dad said that's as long as our backyard," Daniel added.

Pamela rolled her eyes. "Haven't you ever been to the science center before?" she asked.

No one answered. Abby was pleased that the others had decided to ignore Pamela too. That mean part of her felt it was only fair because of the way Pamela was acting. Abby looked for a moment at Pamela, then turned to Andrew and smiled, saying, "Six-inch teeth? That's half a foot!"

"I know! They were monsters. So cool," he said, stepping out of line to stand beside Abby. Pamela's face made a disgusted look. She stepped two feet away.

Abby didn't care. Emma and Lindsay had turned around, and they didn't seem to be annoyed by Andrew or Daniel. Abby was happy that they were all just as excited as she was.

They made their way down the path through the dinosaurs. The ceiling was very high because the dinosaurs were so tall. Along with the dinosaurs, there were big fake trees and ferns. There were also little stuffed animals that had been placed to look like they were hiding from the dinosaurs.

"Stegosaurus is so cool," Abby said. "Look at all the plates on its back."

"Yeah, look at the spikes on its tail. They gave it protection," Andrew said.

"I wish I could take one home," Daniel said.

Abby looked around and saw that Pamela wasn't near them anymore. She moved a few feet out of line and stood on tiptoes to get a better view. *Where did she go?* Abby thought. She didn't want to get in trouble for being caught without a partner.

Finally, Abby spotted her near the triceratops. Pamela was sitting by herself on the floor, writing in her notebook. Abby wondered how Pamela had managed to get so far ahead of the line without either of the teachers noticing. Abby walked toward her.

"Can I sit down?" she asked Pamela.

"If you want to," Pamela answered, staring at her notebook.

"Why are you acting like you don't like the science center?" Abby asked.

"Why are you acting like Andrew is your best friend?"

"I'm not," Abby said. "But I think he is my friend. He's not that bad."

"Well, he wants you to be his girlfriend," Pamela said, looking into Abby's face. Abby was afraid Pamela was going to cry.

"Well, I don't want to be his girlfriend," she said. "I want to be your friend and his friend. Let's not fight. We can still have fun today, even if Andrew is around." Abby touched Pamela's arm and gave it a little tug. She felt sorry that she had made Pamela feel left out.

"I'm sorry I said mean things back there," Pamela said. "I do like the science center, and the dinosaurs."

"I'm sorry, too," Abby said. "Come on, we should get up and start writing in our notebooks."

"You're right," Pamela said. "Will you go back to allosaurus with me? I haven't written any facts yet."

"Sure, let's go," Abby said, pulling her friend up beside her. "Follow me!" Abby led Pamela down the path. A few times, they had to duck or take a longer route to avoid a teacher. Both of them giggled at the strange looks they got from kids who were not part of the third grade class from Woodlawn Elementary. Abby felt a rush of relief and happiness pass through her. The mean part of her had gone away. She and Pamela had made up, and now they could enjoy Dinosaur Day together.

The Mangled Mirror Tragedy

written by Jennifer Tkocs
illustrated by Sean Ricciardi

My mother is going to ship me off to boarding school, I thought. The left side mirror of her brand-new Subaru Legacy lay on the ground at my feet.

"It's just a mirror," my friend Tammy said.

"Easy for you to say," I told her. "It's not the mirror on your mom's car!"

Tammy turned the mirror over with the toe of her sneaker. "Well, I think it was worth it just to see your slap shot."

Moments before the tragedy, we had been playing hockey in my driveway. We've done this since first grade; it wasn't anything new. This was just the first time that my mom had parked her brand-new car in the driveway. After watching a TV program about the environment, she had decided to take the bus to work for a change.

"If you were a better goalie, this wouldn't have happened," I said to Tammy.

"Relax, Staci. I know how to fix this," Tammy assured me. "It'll be easy. Your mom will never know!"

Before I could stop her, Tammy darted through the open door to my garage. I could hear her rummaging around in my dad's toolbox. "Don't mess anything up!" I called. "He won't be home until it's dark, but he'll still know someone touched his stuff!"

After a few minutes, Tammy emerged from the garage. She held up a tube of high-strength Gorilla Glue. "Your parents won't be home until at least 5:00. The glue will be dry by then!"

"I'm not so sure about this," I said. "Maybe I should just tell my mom when she comes home."

"Trust me," Tammy said.

I watched as Tammy slathered glue on the mirror. It didn't look so great. It was a little wobbly and hanging at a strange angle.

"Just as good as new," Tammy said. "But I have to run."

"You're leaving me?"

Tammy shrugged. "I promised my mum I'd be home between 4 and 4:30."

"All right," I said. "Thanks for... helping." I didn't want to seem ungrateful. Tammy was only trying to keep me out of trouble, after all. I was the one who had knocked off the mirror.

I went inside after Tammy left and waited anxiously at the window for my parents to come home from work. They arrived at 5:15 and waved to our neighbor, Mrs. Tomkins. Mrs. Tomkins always kept an eye on me when I got home from school. I was glad she'd been paying more attention to her episodes of Family Feud than to me this afternoon.

When my parents came inside, I tried to pretend everything was just fine.

The first thing my mom said to me was, "Let me tell you—I am never riding that bus again!"

That was when I broke down. "Mom, your new car. I… I ruined it."

"What are you talking about, honey?" she asked. "I just saw it in the driveway. It looks just as perfect today as it did on Tuesday when I brought it home from the dealership."

I gulped. "The mirror," I said. "I knocked the mirror off."

At first, she didn't believe me, but I had to be honest. I went outside with her and showed her Tammy's sloppy fix.

"We should have just told you right away," I said. "But I thought maybe we could fix it."

My mom looked at the mirror. "Well, I think your repair job looks worse than the actual damage would have." She laughed. "Let's make sure Tammy doesn't take up a career at a car shop."

I couldn't believe my mom was laughing. "You aren't mad at me?" I asked. "You aren't going to ship me off to boarding school?"

"Never!" she said. "I will recommend that you avoid home repairs in the future. And you should be more careful playing in the driveway when our cars are there. But you tried to fix the problem, and you were honest about it when you couldn't. That's what counts."

I felt relieved. "I'll be more careful from now on, I promise," I said.

"I know you will," my mom said. "Now let's get some dinner and find an auto body shop that can remove Gorilla Glue."

Ingroy and the Walrus of Udlam: Introduction 1

written by Summer York

The tiny village of Udlam sat in the farthest regions of the Arctic. Its inhabitants had endured that icy landscape for a thousand years. Life in Udlam had barely changed since the first group of brave walrus hunters had settled along the harsh coastline. Young Ingroy would soon follow in his ancestors' footsteps. He would become a walrus hunter and member of the tribe. First, though, he had to prove himself as a man. He had to complete the challenge of the great walrus hunt.

Ingroy and the Walrus of Udlam: Introduction 2

written by Summer York

Young Ingroy sat among the weathered men around the blazing fire. He listened with wide eyes as the gray-haired chief told stories of great walrus hunts. To the people of the tiny ice village of Udlam, the walrus was much more than a source of food. The walrus was a mystical creature. It had magical powers connected to the spirit world. To kill a walrus was a transformative act. It allowed a boy to enter manhood. Listening to the elders' tales, Ingroy could scarcely imagine the journey upon which he would soon embark.

Ingroy and the Walrus of Udlam: Introduction 3

written by Summer York

Ingroy sharply inhaled the icy wind. It bit his skin and took his breath, but he dared not make a sound. Gripping the wooden shaft of his spear, he peered around the jagged rock. He saw the massive figure casting a long shadow on the frozen lake. It was waiting, motionless. Its huge nostrils flared as it tried to catch his scent. Ingroy sank back on his heels and silently exhaled a puff of air, his stomach in knots. He felt young and terribly alone, but there was no turning back now.

Stella's Missing Bear

written by Jennifer Tkocs

My favorite stuffed bear was gone. I had just gotten home from school after Show-and-Tell Day, but my bear had somehow not made it back with me.

I opened my backpack for the seventh time and searched inside. *He has to be in here!* I thought. In fact, I remembered putting him in my backpack right after show-and-tell ended.

I walked into the kitchen where my mom was peeling potatoes for dinner. "Mom! Mom, Bear is gone!"

"What do you mean?" she asked. "Shouldn't he be on your bed?"

My face fell. "No," I said. "I took him to school with me this morning."

"Stella, didn't we talk about this?" Mom crossed her arms. "You are supposed to leave your important toys here while you go to school."

"I know, Mom. But today was a really special show-and-tell. I needed to have him there!" I already felt bad enough that Bear was gone. Now I felt guilty for not listening to my mom too.

"Let's retrace your steps," she suggested. "We'll see if we can find Bear. Where was the last place you saw him?"

"School," I said. "I was the first to present at show-and-tell. Then, I had him at my desk during all the other presentations."

We got into the car and drove back to the school. My teacher was still there, finishing up some paperwork. "Mrs. Jenkins, did I leave my bear here?" I asked.

"I don't think so," she said. "I always tidy the room immediately following the end of class. I would have seen him if he was still here."

"All right, thanks," I said glumly. "We'll keep looking."

We checked the sidewalks on the route that I walked home. There was no sign of Bear. I felt like I was going to cry. "We'll never find him!" I told my mom.

"Before you get too upset, let's remember a couple of things," she said. "You were only at school and then walked home. He couldn't have gone far."

"But we would have seen him by now," I said. "If he'd gotten lost anywhere between me leaving school and getting to our house, we would have seen him."

"Maybe," she said. "But don't forget that we put your name and address on the tag inside Bear's shirt. If someone found him, they may bring him to our house."

She had a point. "I'll try to be patient," I said.

Two whole weeks went by with no sign of Bear. Every day, I checked the front steps, hoping someone had dropped him off. I was ready to give up hope.

Then, as I arrived home from school one day, I saw a large package on our front porch. "Mom!" I called as I ran into the house. "What's this box?"

We opened the box and, sure enough, Bear was inside. With him was an envelope marked "Stella" on the front. "What's this?" I wondered.

Inside the envelope was a stack of photos. Bear was in each one! Here he was at the Eiffel Tower. Here he was with a paw up, waving from Big Ben. "Bear!" I exclaimed. "Where have you been?"

Underneath the photos was a note. "Dear Stella," it read. "I found your bear on the sidewalk outside of my house. He must have fallen out of your bag. I would have returned him right away, but my husband and I were already late to go to the airport for our European vacation. We thought that perhaps your bear could use an adventure. My apologies for having him out so long, but I hope you enjoy seeing his vacation!"

The note was signed by Mrs. Mertz, one of our neighbors. She and Mr. Mertz were retired and traveled all the time.

"Bear came back!" I told my mom. "And he's been halfway across the world!"

"I'm sure he had fun," Mom said. "Still, I hope you learn a lesson from this."

"I'll be more careful with my toys," I promised, "especially this little world traveler!"

– 9 –

Rising Action in *Bunnicula*

written by Summer York

Bunnicula, by Deborah and James Howe, is the funny yet suspenseful story of a rabbit that seems to be a vampire. When the Monroe family goes to a showing of the movie *Dracula*, they find a small black and white rabbit in the theater. They bring it home and name it Bunnicula. However, odd things start to happen after Bunnicula's arrival, and Harold the dog and Chester the cat must work together to solve the mystery.

Chester is a well-read cat who enjoys mystery and horror stories. He immediately notices strange things about Bunnicula. The rabbit has a black spot on its back in the shape of Dracula's cape. It also has pointy, fang-like teeth. It even sleeps all day and is awake at night. This makes Chester worried.

Chester's concern grows when the family begins finding white vegetables in the kitchen. A tomato, lettuce, carrots, and a zucchini are all found drained of their juices. Each vegetable has two tiny holes, like fang marks. Chester notes that vampires are known to drain their victims.

Chester and Harold become convinced that Bunnicula is a vampire rabbit. They decide to take matters into their own hands. First, Chester puts garlic all over the house, because vampires do not like garlic. Next, he tries to pound a stake into Bunnicula.

However, he mistakenly uses a steak instead of a stake. Finally, Chester tries to starve Bunnicula in an effort to get rid of him.

The suspense mounts as the story's rising action builds. Is Bunnicula really a vampire rabbit? Can Harold and Chester protect the family? What will happen to Bunnicula? These questions keep the reader guessing until the end of the story.

Works Cited

"Comprehension Questions – *Bunnicula: A Rabbit Tale of Mystery*." *Rise to Reading*, www.risetoreading.com/2014/03/29/comprehension-questions-bunnicula/. Accessed 11 Feb. 2017.

Howe, Deborah and James Howe. *Bunnicula: A Rabbit-Tale of Mystery.* Simon & Schuster, 1979.

Shore, Amy. "A Guide for Using *Bunnicula: A Rabbit Tale of Mystery* in the Classroom." *AliceChristie.org*, alicechristie.org/workshops/imagine/bunnicula-whole-packet.pdf. Accessed 11 Feb. 2017.

Jay and the Race

written by Sarah Marino
illustrated by Dion Williams

Jay Patanga and his best friend, Garrett Brook, were sitting in the lounge of the Miwok Rancheria rec center, doing homework, when they noticed someone lurking in the doorway. It was a kid who looked to be about their age, with sleek, shiny black hair that covered half of his round face and did not stop until his shoulders. He kept standing there, glancing around the room, and every now and then looking directly at Jay or Garrett.

"Are you looking for someone?" Jay asked. He had never seen this kid before and thought he looked lost. He had a bad feeling, though, that the "someone" this kid was looking for was himself. When the kid didn't answer, Jay introduced himself and asked, "What's your name?"

"I know who you are," he said, stepping into the room. "I'm Rubin."

"Do I know you?" Jay asked.

"Yeah, you don't look familiar," Garrett said.

"It doesn't matter. I was sent here. I'm challenging you to a running race, one mile, at the festival this Saturday. The winner will become the leader of the next generation of Miwoks."

Jay and Garrett looked at each other, and then began to chuckle.

"Who are you, man?" Jay asked. "Are you serious?"

"It's not a joke, and I'd suggest you stop laughing." Rubin suddenly closed his eyes and bowed his head slightly, and then a huge, old dictionary toppled off of a shelf near their table, almost crashing onto Garrett's foot.

Jay was a bit stunned. Luckily for him, running was something he was good at. He wasn't sure who Rubin was, or what this "being leader of the next generation" stuff was about, but he was always up for a race. He wanted some more information, though.

"I will race you. But I'd like to know who sent you here." Jay could not keep the tone of fear from creeping into his voice.

"You will be safe in the race," Rubin began. "My mother is a medicine woman of the ancient Miwoks. We live in the mountains, close to the Great Spirit. This race has been foretold. You do not need to have fear."

Jay was not sure if these words eased his mind, but he was happy to have learned more, at least. He knew of the medicine men and women, the healers. They were harmless. Most modern Miwoks did not believe in them. Jay's great grandfather had been one, so he'd heard many stories. Part of him believed.

"Okay, what time on Saturday and where, exactly?" he asked.

"At noon. We will meet at the end of Eagle Creek, next to the tree of the vulture." And with that, Rubin turned and walked out of the room.

Garrett looked at Jay. "Wow, that was bizarre. The next leader? If it's you versus that guy, I think you'd better be sure and win this one."

Neither of them knew if what Rubin had said was true, but it seemed, for some strange reason, like the truth. It was almost too weird not to be.

***

Jay had a dream that night: he was walking alone through Eagle Creek around nightfall. There was almost no noise except for his feet stepping through the water in the shallow stream. Even though there was little light and some of the stones he stepped on were slippery, he did not look down, because he knew he would not fall. He kept walking and heard a voice to his left and ahead, say, "This will be your race. I will help you. If you wish to succeed, however, your whole heart must be devoted to winning. It will not be an easy race. You will need focus, determination, trust, and belief in yourself." Jay had stopped walking and the voice stopped. He heard what sounded like very light footsteps. Then, a small coyote emerged from the darkness into his line of vision. It nodded at him.

"You?" Jay asked. He did not get a response, but he was almost sure the coyote had smiled before it disappeared.

***

Since he had turned six, and his grandfather had told him that every Miwok had a great animal spirit inside him- or herself, Jay had been obsessed. He wanted to see his animal spirit. He wanted to speak to it. What animal was it? When would he meet it? On his birthday each year, he would think: Maybe this will be the year that the spirit will show itself to me. Now that he was ten, he felt the same. His grandfather had told him that you could feel the spirit when you most needed it, but that it did not often show itself. The animal spirit was connected to the Great Spirit, found in all things in the universe. His grandfather had said that only persons whose hearts were ready would ever see their animal spirits.

So, when he woke the next morning, Jay wondered if the coyote that had appeared in his dream was his animal spirit. He certainly didn't think his "heart was ready," and he wasn't even sure what that meant, anyway. His cousin, Chris, said he was crazy and spirit animals were a bogus story told by the grandparents to scare the kids. But Jay thought his cousin was wrong. Even though Chris was three years older, Jay was old enough to know that Chris didn't know everything.

He was almost sure the coyote was his animal spirit. He wanted to believe it. He had a race to run tomorrow, and if his Miwok ancestry could help him win the race, in whatever form, he would be grateful. The summer sun in Sacramento was often not a pleasant thing. And this was the annual summer festival, when Miwoks came from all across the country to see their families in the region where the first tribe had lived. He ached at the thought that he might lose in front of all of his fellow tribe members.

Jay did not think anyone but Garrett knew about the race, but he was sure people would find out soon enough. He decided not to tell his parents. He knew he needed to win the race on his own.

***

On Saturday, Jay and Garrett arrived fifteen minutes early. The race was in the Sierra foothills. They would be on mostly flat land, but the little rolling hills would be all around, with the great low mountains of the Sierra Nevada rising in the east. The smell of dry, July earth was overpowering; it was almost like being in a barn full of hay.

Rubin was waiting for them beside a buckeye tree in which a vulture sat on one of the low branches.

"Good luck, Jay. I know you'll be fine," Garrett said. "Look, I hope you don't mind, but I invited a few others, okay? I didn't want to stand here and wait by myself," he said, smiling. "And I thought you could use the support."

Jay looked around and saw their friends Fiona and Arnie walking toward them. They said hello and wished him luck.

"I guess he doesn't have anyone to come and watch," Garrett said quietly, looking toward Rubin.

"Yeah, I guess not. I should probably go," Jay said. He walked toward Rubin and felt his stomach begin to twist and his heart begin to knock at his chest. He tried to control his breathing.

Rubin was wearing a traditional-looking Miwok shirt and blue jeans. His hair hung in his face.

"Glad you made it," Rubin said. "It's almost time. Half a mile up, and then we turn around. We run to the cypress trees, just where the creek begins to curve toward the mountains."

"Why do you make the rules?" Jay said. "Is there something I should know?"

"I've already told you what you need to know. I've been sent to complete this task, to race with you. The winner will lead the next generation of Miwoks. I wish you luck. We will begin when the vulture cries." Rubin took his place at what Jay assumed was a starting line. Jay followed and stood beside him. He could hear Garrett, Fiona, and Arnie talking several yards away. He felt better knowing they were there.

In the next moment, the vulture gave a shriek and they were off. Jay began running and he saw Rubin glide ahead by a few feet. He remembered what the coyote had said: his whole heart had to be devoted to winning. Jay summoned strength from his heart. He felt power in his legs carrying him and air flooding his lungs. He surged forward.

Soon they were at the cypress trees, the halfway mark. They were about even and turned at nearly the same time. The sun had become an enemy, beating down on them from a cloudless sky. Sweat dripped from Jay's brow into his eyes. The salt stung; he blinked and used his arm to wipe his face. Rubin did not even appear to be sweating. Jay began to wonder about this

– 13 –

and realized he was losing focus. Rubin was now many yards ahead.

Then, he saw it. On his right, the coyote jogged several paces ahead of him, just up to Rubin's place. *Your whole heart. Keep up with me*, Jay heard a voice in his head say. He stared at the coyote and felt his heart rise. He'd been right. His animal spirit. He wiped away the sweat again, and, suddenly, the white sunlight, the shrubs and dirt, and Rubin disappeared. Jay could no longer see his friends ahead. All he saw was darkness, but he could still make out the coyote jogging ahead of him, followed by a dim bluish-white trail of light. It looked like the tails of the shooting stars he'd seen while lying in the backyard on late summer nights, but the light didn't fade. It seemed to get brighter. Jay wanted to reach it. He knew there was no reason to be afraid. He just had to keep moving as fast as he could. He looked at the coyote and raced to catch up with it. He felt his legs pounding and his arms pumping as if he were no longer in control. He pushed harder and reached the coyote. Then he pushed with every bit of strength he had and all at once the sunlight returned; the coyote and its trail of light were gone. He had rushed ahead, passing Rubin, and was standing beside Garrett. He'd won. He bent over and took several deep breaths.

"The coyote," he said softly, looking back to the finish line, but only Rubin was there.

"You've done a very good thing," said Rubin, approaching him. "You are the next leader of the Miwok, and all of the people will know. I am glad to have met you." Rubin held out his hand. Jay shook it, not sure of what to say.

"Listen, thank you," Jay began, "but I don't know what all of this means."

"It will become real for you very soon. The test had to come now. You will lead when they need you. Do not worry. You have done well." He smiled for the first time. "Well, I must get back."

"Thank you again, then," Jay said. He and the others watched as Rubin crossed Eagle Creek and began walking up a road that led toward the mountains.

"Every time we see that guy, things get stranger and stranger," Garrett said. "I'm glad you won, Jay. Congratulations!"

"Yes, congrats!" Fiona said. "Was all of that true, about being the next leader when they need you?"

"I guess it is. He said it would become real very soon. Maybe we should get back to the festival."

They looked to the west, where the town was, and could see people celebrating in the streets. They began their walk. Jay could feel the coyote still with him. He looked around but knew he wouldn't see it. He was sure there would be other times when he would need it again. He was happy now just to walk with his friends toward an exciting day and a future he would give his whole heart to.

Story Climax in *Mulan*

written by Summer York

Mulan depicts the adventure of a young Chinese woman who disguises herself as a man. She takes her father's place in the army. Later, she fights against the invading Huns. Mulan's secret is discovered after a fierce battle. Afterward, her comrades leave her in the mountains and travel to the Imperial City. The climax of the story occurs during their victory celebration. The Huns return and attack the city. Shan Yu, leader of the Hun army, kidnaps the emperor. Shan Yu holds the emperor captive in the palace. Mulan and her friends must outsmart the Huns and rescue the emperor. They think quickly and get the emperor to safety. Then, Shan Yu turns his rage on Mulan. With help from Mushu, Mulan's guardian dragon, Shan Yu is finally killed by an exploding firework on the roof of the palace. The emperor is safe, and Mulan is deemed a hero.

Works Cited

Bancroft, Tony and Barry Cook, directors. *Mulan*. Walt Disney Pictures, 1998.

The Old Rabbit and the Sly Fox: An Aesop's Fable

adapted by Jill Fisher
illustrated by Dion Williams

An old rabbit lived alone in the woods. Her home was a burrow deep under the ground. She'd had a long life and had collected many beautiful things. She kept them in her burrow and treasured each object. Some of them were sparkly and others were big and heavy. She loved to look at them and admire the beauty of each object. Each one had a priceless value to the elderly rabbit.

One summer morning, when the old rabbit opened her eyes, she could not see! She was so upset. She did not know what to do. She shouted out, "I cannot see! I need help!"

Right outside the old rabbit's burrow was a sly fox. He heard her cry for help and went running inside her home. He could not believe his eyes when he saw all of her treasures. He said, "I am here to help you." Really, though, he had an evil plan in mind.

The sly fox told the old rabbit, "I will help you gain your eyesight if you promise me a large amount of money when you can see again." The rabbit was so upset and desperate that she thanked the helpful fox and agreed to the plan. The fox laughed to himself because the trusting old rabbit had fallen into his tricky trap.

He quickly got to work. Every day the fox stopped by the rabbit's burrow to put cream on her eyes. Each day as he left the burrow he grabbed one of her special treasures. He was stealing her things little by little. The fox thought that no one would ever know the difference.

Soon, the clever fox had taken all of the old rabbit's special treasures. Once he had stolen all that she had, he put the special potion on her eyes. The next day, her eyes were healed. The old rabbit could not believe what she saw. "My eyes must be playing a trick on me, because I do not see any of my beautiful treasures," she said.

Not long after, the fox stopped by the burrow. He said, "I am here to collect my payment like you promised."

The old rabbit look around her burrow once more and saw none of her things. "I refuse to pay you any money," she replied.

The fox insisted the rabbit go before the leader of the forest, the great owl. The fox told the owl, "The old rabbit promised me a large amount of money for fixing her eyesight. However, she is now better and will not pay." The wise owl listened carefully.

When it was the old rabbit's turn to speak, she stood and spoke clearly. "The fox is speaking the truth," she said. "We did have a deal. I promised him a large amount of money if he fixed my eyesight. However, when I looked around my burrow I saw none of my special treasures. Therefore, I must still be blind. If I continue to be blind, I do not have to pay."

The owl agreed with the old rabbit. He said that she did not have to pay the sly fox. Then he ordered the fox to return the special treasures to the old rabbit. The owl told the fox, "He who plays tricks must be prepared to take a joke."

Falling Action in *Sleeping Beauty*

written by Summer York

In *Sleeping Beauty*, the falling action occurs after Prince Philip defeats the evil Queen Maleficent. With the evil queen gone, Prince Philip searches the castle for Princess Aurora. The evil queen put a spell on the princess. The spell made Aurora prick her finger on a spinning wheel. This put her to sleep. The only thing that can awaken her is a kiss from her true love, Prince Philip. The prince finds Aurora and kneels beside her bed. He gives her true love's kiss. It awakens her and the rest of the sleeping kingdom. The kingdom is restored! Princess Aurora and Prince Philip greet their subjects. They dance together. As their parents and friends watch, Princess Aurora and Prince Philip prepare to live happily ever after.

Work Cited

Geronimi, Clyde, director. *Sleeping Beauty*. Walt Disney Productions, 1959.

How Sofia Tamed the Dragon

written by Summer York
illustrated by David Rushbrook

The faraway kingdom of Fairywood was a land of magic. It was a place where brave knights battled fierce dragons and rescued lovely princesses. A place where wicked witches plotted foul deeds, and where powerful sorcerers and enchanted fairies used their magic to defeat evil. Such stories have been told and retold in many places, but all of them were born in Fairywood. That is how they became known as fairy tales.

In the land of Fairywood there lived a magical fairy princess named Sofia. She was beautiful, with golden hair as soft as silk and lips as pink as a posy. She was kind and fair, and she was also very brave. Everyone in the kingdom loved her.

Sofia lived with her old uncle, a powerful sorcerer named Mervin. Sofia was devoted to her uncle and he loved her dearly. Over the years, Mervin taught his niece everything he knew about magic. Because they were good and just people, they only used their magic for good.

But on the other side of the kingdom, there lived an ugly, wicked witch. She was very powerful, but she used her magic for evil. Everyone in Fairywood was afraid of her. Many years ago, Mervin had banished her from Fairywood. It was said that she was very angry and was hiding in her castle in the mountains while she plotted her revenge.

Word came to the kingdom that the witch had kidnapped a handsome prince from another kingdom. She locked him in the highest tower in her castle. The castle was said to be guarded by a huge, fire-breathing dragon. Many brave knights from the prince's land had tried to defeat the dragon and rescue the prince, but all had failed. The people feared he would be the witch's prisoner forever.

"Uncle, have you heard the story?" Sofia asked Mervin. "The witch is holding Prince Edward prisoner in her tower."

"I have heard, niece," Mervin replied. "It seems that her time in the mountains has not changed her evil ways."

"I think we should do something," Sofia said.

Mervin was not surprised that his niece wanted to help. "But Sofia," he said, "the dragon is very dangerous. Many knights have tried to defeat it and have failed. What can you do?"

Sofia thought for a moment. "Well," she said, "we have something that none of the knights had: magic! We don't have to defeat the dragon. We just need to tame it."

"A magic spell!" Mervin exclaimed. "We will come up with a spell that will make the dragon as tame as a kitten."

With their plan in place, Mervin and Sofia began to work on the magic spell. They worked for three days and three nights. On the third night, the spell was finished.

"Now we must prepare for our journey," Sofia said, packing some food into a sack.

"Alas, I am too old to travel that far," Mervin said sadly. "You must do this alone."

"But Uncle Mervin," Sofia protested, "what if I forget the spell?" She was afraid. "I am not big enough and strong enough to protect myself if my magic fails."

"Sofia," Mervin began, "sometimes what is on the inside is more important than what is on the outside." He hugged her tightly. "You have everything you need to succeed. You just have to believe in yourself the way that I believe in you."

With Mervin's comforting words, Sofia began her long journey to the witch's castle. She rode her trusted friend, a magical unicorn named Star. Together, they left the safe walls of the kingdom behind and headed for the deep forest.

Once inside the forest, it was as dark as night. Star used her bright horn to light the way. They traveled for many days, only stopping to sleep on the soft ground. Eventually, they came to the end of the forest and out onto an open plain. They could see the dark mountains up ahead.

"Come on, old friend," Sofia said to Star. "It's not far now." They crossed the plain and were soon at the base of the mountain. They found a small foot path and began to climb upward. When they were about halfway up the mountain, they heard the horrible cry of the dragon.

"We must be getting close," Sofia whispered. "You stay here and wait for me." She hugged Star's neck. "I'll be back soon," Sofia told her.

The princess stepped out from under the trees and saw the castle. She looked up at the tower reaching toward the sky. That must be where Prince Edward is, she thought. All of a sudden, a huge shadow fell over her. She felt the hot, fiery breath of the dragon. It flew over her and landed between her and the castle. It glared at her, its eyes glowing as brightly as the sun. But Sofia was not afraid. She knew what she had to do.

Just as the dragon took a step toward her, Sofia began to sing. She sang softly at first, then her voice grew strong. She was singing the spell that Uncle Mervin had taught her. The dragon stopped its attack and froze in place. It pricked up its ears. It was listening to Sofia sing.

"It's working!" Sofia thought hopefully. She continued the spell. The dragon sat down, still listening to the song. As the spell came to an end, the dragon lay down and wagged its tail like a happy dog. Sofia carefully walked up to it. Reaching out her hand, she began to pet the dragon's huge head.

"That's a good dragon," Sofia said. It liked when she scratched behind its ears. "Now, dragon," she said, "I need your help." Sofia climbed onto the dragon's back. "I need you to fly me up to the tower. We're going to rescue the prince." The dragon obeyed. It stretched its giant wings and flew Sofia up to the tiny window in the witch's tower.

As Sofia peered in the window, she saw the prince. He looked up, startled. "Prince Edward," Sofia said softly. "Don't be afraid. I'm here to rescue you."

"But how did you get past the dragon?" the prince asked.

"Just a little magic," Sofia said with a smile. "It's a tame dragon now." Together they climbed onto the dragon's back and flew back down to the ground. Star came out to greet them.

"It's not often that a princess rescues a prince," Edward said. "Thank you."

They all went back to Fairywood together. Word soon followed that the evil witch was in a fit of rage. She could not believe that the prince had been rescued and that her dragon was gone. It was said that she was still hiding in the mountains, plotting her next evil plan. But no one in Fairywood let the witch's mood ruin their celebration. Uncle Mervin was so proud of his niece. And the people of the kingdom were happy that they had a friendly dragon to protect them. Maybe they would all meet the evil witch again someday, but that is for another fairy tale to tell.

Abstract Nouns

written by Mark Weimer

A noun is a person, place, or thing. People, places, and things are **concrete nouns**. They are objects out in the world. **Abstract nouns** are things that your five senses cannot detect. The word *abstract* describes a thing that exists in your thoughts. This means that you cannot see, hear, smell, taste, or touch it. Abstract nouns are thoughts in your mind. They are often ideas, emotions, and qualities.

It is helpful to begin with what an abstract noun is *not*. Most nouns are concrete nouns; they refer to people, places, and things. Anything that you can see, hear, smell, taste, or touch is a concrete noun. Foods, cities, cars, books, pencils, and trees are concrete nouns.

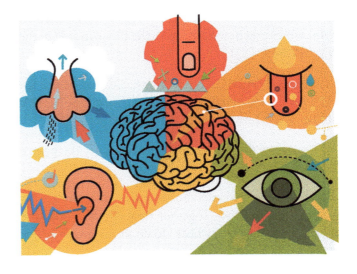

An abstract noun is something that is not out in the world. It is a thought that you cannot detect with the five senses. An idea is an abstract noun. Emotions are also abstract nouns. You can talk about being angry or full of love, but can you touch anger? Can you actually eat love? Of course not. Anger and love are emotions in your mind. Qualities such as bravery and courage are also abstract nouns. You can always say that somebody has bravery, but you cannot go to the store and buy a can of bravery. You cannot go visit courage. These human qualities are abstract nouns, and you cannot see, hear, smell, taste, or touch them.

Abstract nouns are used for many reasons. They make writing more interesting. They also allow readers to relate to the writing. It would be hard to write without being able to use abstract nouns. You would not be able to write about ideas, which is one of the primary reasons to write. You could not write about fear, love, humor, truth, opinion, or many other subjects. Writing would be dry, boring, and barely enjoyable to read. Abstract nouns allow readers to better relate to what the author is writing. As the author, you can share written feelings, concepts, and ideas with your readers. This makes a piece of writing more powerful. Imagine a story written about a dream. You can relate because you have had dreams. You know what it is like to dream. Imagine a story with characters who succeed at times and fail at others. You can relate because you have succeeded and failed too. Readers can better understand and *feel* the emotions of characters when characters are angry, sad, happy, frustrated, excited, disappointed, or amazed. The more a reader can relate to writing, the more the reader can understand and enjoy a story. Unlike concrete nouns, abstract nouns allow authors to discuss experiences that are not limited to sight, sound, smell, taste, and touch.

Postcards from Pismo: A Report

written by Mark Weimer
illustrated by Dion Williams

Postcards from Pismo is a story about Felix Maldonado, a boy from Pismo Beach. Pismo Beach is a town in California. Felix lives by the ocean with his mom, dad, and brother, Quin. The story is told through a series of letters and postcards. Felix writes to Lieutenant Marcus Greene, a soldier in Afghanistan. It all begins as part of a school project. Felix and Marcus continue to write to each other for several months after. They form a strong friendship during this time.

Felix begins to send more letters when Quin makes a big change in his life. One day, Quin quits his job. This is upsetting to Felix and Quin's parents. It becomes worse when Quin explains why he quit: He has enlisted in the National Guard. It sets off a huge fight. Felix grows very worried about Quin. He begins to write even more to Marcus. He knows that Marcus can help him deal with his worries. Marcus can explain what it is like being a soldier.

As Felix works through his fears about Quin, he decides to overcome some other fears as well. He begins to go places he typically avoids because of a bully named Roger Batista. One of these places is the arcade along the Promenade. The Promenade is a paved strip overlooking the beach. It offers lot of shops and things to do.

One day, as Felix is playing a video game, Roger Batista and his pals, Lupe and Kenneth, squirt Felix in the back with nasty pier water. Everybody makes fun of Felix because of the fishy smell. He has to take off his wet, stinky shirt. Shirtless, he rides his bike home to the chants of "Fish Stick." Getting squirted eventually leads to a fight between Felix and Roger in school. Felix

punches Roger in the nose and makes his nose bleed. Felix feels terrible, especially when he realizes how cruelly Roger's father treats his son.

Felix is suspended from school. To make matters worse, he learns that Marcus has been injured in Afghanistan. It is everything that Felix fears will eventually happen to Quin. Marcus explains to Felix that he is being cared for in a hospital in Washington, DC. This helps calm Felix's fears about Quin, from whom he has yet to hear. Felix knows that Quin could get injured if he is deployed. Felix's continued correspondence with Marcus leads him to start a new school project. He asks the entire fifth grade class to create and send postcards to the soldiers in the hospital where Marcus is staying.

Works Cited

Scotto, Michael. *Postcards from Pismo*. Midlandia Press, 2012.

Augusta Rain: Secret Superhero

written by Augusta Rain
transcribed by Sarah Marino
illustrated by Charles Kuehn

That day was an odd one in lots of ways. The sky was a pearly gray and was growing darker by the hour. The sun was lost behind a thick foam of clouds. I was beside the lake, trying to catch fish. I was never any good at fishing, but I enjoyed sitting on the dock, listening to the water swirl around and the birds sing. In my little town, there wasn't much else for a fourteen-year-old girl to do.

The fish had not come around the dock much, but the one that finally flitted into view was like no fish I'd seen before. It was a trout with a reddish stripe down its back. It had two fins on each side and three eyes.

About the same time that this fish appeared, the sky began to change. It darkened to a deep gray and I could hear thunder in the distance. I wanted to get the fish, to take it to show my parents. Something was definitely wrong with it, but I had no idea what. Scrambling to get my pole, I leaned over the dock. To my surprise, the fish didn't move. It just hung out there, and I could have sworn it was looking at me with all three of its eyes. Then it poked its head out of the water. I jumped back. It bobbed down and then came back up out of the water again.

Meanwhile, the storm clouds had drifted almost directly above the lake. I paid them no mind. I lay on my stomach and put my arms in the water. As the fish swam to meet me, a loud crack of thunder boomed.

In the same instant, a lightning bolt like a dagger pierced the lake. A silver-blue current ran through the water, stinging the fish, which had, at that point, reached my hands.

The fish lurched up at me and I felt an odd tingling sensation, like when I get the chills reading a really good part of a story. But this tingling was more solid, like an actual electric current was flowing through me. Of course, I learned quickly that the feeling was, indeed, a real current in my veins. The lightning. The fish. The lake. I was never the same again.

From that day on, I could do things that I hadn't been able to do before. For example, I could speak to fish and, sometimes, to other animals. My vision changed as well. I could see acid rain in ponds, lakes, streams, and woods. I could see pesticides in places where they might harm humans and animals. I could see it coating things like a film of motor oil. It became my duty to clean up these places. With a simple head bow and a concentrated request, I could summon pure, clean rain clouds that would evaporate the chemicals and return a clean rain to the land. I could also run extremely fast, like lightning. This was my favorite part.

Most people don't know it, but there are a lot of polluted rivers, lakes, and woods around. The trout that changed me that day had been harmed by acid rain and, somehow, was trying to get my help. Whether it was sheer chance, or part of a larger plan that I could not understand, I'm not sure. I don't question it anymore. It's my life, and I have gradually learned to accept it.

With my new powers, however, came new responsibilities. Part of my role was to educate people, leaving signs here and there. Of course, I had to make sure my powers were pretty much hidden. Even at fourteen, I realized that people would find it odd to see a teenage girl wandering around talking to clouds and rain, cleaning up pollution as if by magic.

It was pretty easy to keep it hidden. I didn't have any strange markings; I didn't turn into an animal. I did get a tiny fish-shaped scar in the palm of my right hand. Otherwise, I didn't really change on the outside in any way. Overall, I looked like a typical teenager. I had blondish-brown hair that I wore in a ponytail. I often wore headphones in the hopes of making people think I was just out for a jog and a stroll, rather than an unusual girl with a mission.

Normally, it would work like this: in the late afternoon or evening, the scar on my hand would begin to tingle. By bedtime, it would build to a slow, almost aching, pulse. That night I would dream of the next place where I was to go. These dreams were as vivid as real life. When I would awaken, I would remember the place like I had certainly been there before, although I knew I had not been. I could close my eyes and see it in perfect detail.

After the dream, the fun would begin. I would go to the woods behind my house and wait until no one was around. Then I'd start jogging, holding a picture in my mind of the place where I needed to be. My speed would pick up without my trying. Soon I'd be running so fast that it felt like my feet weren't touching the ground. I usually got dizzy. In what seemed like seconds, I'd arrive.

I repeated this process countless times, visiting places all over the United States: Tennessee, Louisiana, Wyoming, Ohio, Pennsylvania, Virginia, and more. It could be tiring, but I enjoyed it. I met animals and people and left feeling like I'd made a big improvement in their lives. That was a feeling I came to enjoy, especially as I grew older.

Despite my unusual job, I managed to have a semi-normal life. My missions would usually happen on weekends, and mostly in the summer. I still went to school and managed to keep a few close friends. I didn't tell any friends or my parents because I feared they would make me stop. I realize now that my parents may have been supportive. They were open-minded, if strict, and believed in helping the environment.

Things went swimmingly most times. There was one time, though, that things got tricky. What seemed like a problem at the time became something of a blessing. It was in the Catskill Mountains, in New York. It was a wonderful, sunny day in May. I was eighteen, a month away from my high school graduation. The sun burned white in the sky, which was a sparkling bright blue compared to the green pine trees on the mountains. As lovely as it looked, I knew that within the forest things were not so pretty. I soon found a large pond, a stream, and a forest area that were in need of help.

I met a young black bear and her cubs there. The mother bear told me that the cubs were running fevers and had lost their energy ever since they'd come to these parts and drunk the water. She also told me to look at the trees. They were losing needles and even branches.

Looking back, I remember doing my task with energy, but there was also a sense of sadness that I didn't admit to myself until much later. Seeing these beautiful places badly polluted and the animals and people feeling sickly—it was a lot for a teenager to handle. I was brave, though. I believed that my powers would help them. I believed that I was making it better—if not completely better, then at least mostly better.

The bears had moved on. I was about to take my position and summon the clouds when a voice to my right called out, "Are you lost, miss? You okay?" My heart stopped. I was sure I felt it skip three beats. I turned slowly toward the voice. It was a forest ranger. In a different situation, I would have been happy to see him; however, I was in my situation and I needed to get to work. I had a feeling it was going to be a long day.

"Uh, I'm fine. I live around here. Just out for a hike," I said.

"This is a little far from town to be out for a hike. We don't allow people in this area. It has been polluted. You shouldn't be here," the ranger said.

I was worried that he was angry, but I looked his way again and his face seemed kind. He was handsome and looked not much older than me. He smiled.

"Why don't you come to the office with me and we'll get you home?" he said, stepping closer to me.

"I don't go anywhere with men I don't know," I said.

"Well, I'll show you my badge."

I sighed. I just wanted to do my work and get back home. I knew he would interfere with that plan. I thought about running away; he never would have caught up. But I had to be in that area to summon the clouds. Then I realized that I could try to explain what I was doing, get far enough away to start the process, and then be gone before he could take in what I'd said. I smiled to myself.

"I have work to do here," I said.

"Work?" he asked. He looked at me strangely.

"You can stay if you want to, but I must do it." I jogged away from him and could hear him following. I went close to the edge of the pond and began, head bowed. I stood in silence, waiting, hoping that his presence wouldn't stop the clouds. Oddly, they seemed to come quicker than ever. He stood beside me and watched. The clouds came, evaporated the harmful chemicals and acids, and then rained crystal-clear drops: rain that you could drink; rain that made your hair silky and smelled of clouds and flowers; rain without pollution.

When it was over, I sat down, tired. He came and sat with me.

"Did you... did you just make that happen?" he asked. "There was no rain in the forecast today."

– 26 –

I nodded. At the time, I felt too tired to make up another lie. Looking back, though, I think I'd been hoping to find someone to talk to, to share my secret with.

It turned out Connor was that person. He was comforting, and we made a plan to work together with the rangers to do whatever we could. It was my gift and I had to use it.

It has been amazing, fulfilling work. I may not have chosen it, but I'm grateful for whatever happened that day with the trout. Working with the rangers made me realize that even people without my abilities can help in dramatic ways. We can all make the water and earth safer for ourselves and the animals with which we share it.

Connor and I married eventually, and we have three children now. Someday when they're older, they will hear this story too.

The Fisherman and the Little Fish

adapted by Sarah Marino
illustrated by Dion Williams

In a little village by a lake, there lived a hardworking fisherman named Walter. Just as he did every morning, Walter awoke today and washed and dressed before having a breakfast of oatmeal with his wife and children. He left the warmth of his home and began his walk to the shore of the lake. There, he would fish on his own dock, made of pine, which he had built himself.

Walter and his family were not rich, but they got along well enough. They always had food on the table, whether fish that Walter could not sell at the market or vegetables from his wife's garden.

It was December. The temperature was just barely above freezing. Walter walked along the sidewalk on the edge of town, toward the lake. Tiny white specks of snow flew around him in the cold, misty air. He was thankful that he had taken his wife's advice to put on his old wool snow hat.

As he arrived at the dock, the sun began to rise on the eastern edge of the lake. The sky was glowing bright pink, fading into white, above the tip of the round edge of the sun. Tim was already set up at his dock, which was, in Walter's opinion, too close to his own. "Figures," Walter thought. "Even on the first cold day, he had to beat me to it."

"Ah, good morning, Walter," said Tim. "Fine, fine morning, isn't it?" Tim was shorter than Walter and a good bit heavier. He had large ears that were always red and brown hair cut close to his head.

"Good morning," Walter replied. "Yes, a bit chilly, but fine." It wasn't that Walter disliked Tim. He would simply prefer to fish without so much talking, to listen to the ripples of the water as the wind moved it and to the gulls and ospreys that flew around the lake. Tim, on the other hand, enjoyed a good chat at all times.

Walter had learned how to ignore him in a kind way. He gave short answers, some longer if he was interested in a topic. Tim had come to accept that Walter was just a different type, a quiet sort of fellow. This was fine with Walter.

Walter prepared his pole, line, and bait, and cast off. He sometimes used a net if the water was calm and the birds were far off in the distance. This was when the smaller catfish and trout would come close to the dock to feed on the grasses near the shore.

"I already caught a nice one," Tim said. "Look at this." He held up a ten-inch bass. Its scales were sparkling. It was plump and broad, as if it might burst.

Walter glanced at the fish. He felt a pang of envy that quickly turned to annoyance. He had not caught anything that big in days. He was beginning to wonder whether his skill was fading now that he'd reached middle age. He knew it wasn't a competition. Besides, Tim had five children to feed; Walter only had three.

As Walter turned to see who was at the other docks nearby, he felt a small pull on his line. It was just barely a tug. He reeled in a bit to test it and felt a definite resistance, though it wasn't very strong. He never announced his catches to Tim, usually because Tim would be commentating on the entire scene as soon as he realized Walter had something. Tim would chatter away like a regular sports announcer.

He brought his line in and found a little fish there. The fish was light blue with a yellow line down the side of it, below its fin. Walter took hold of it and heard the fish begin to speak: "Please, sir, I beg you, let me return to the lake. I am a little fish and am surely of no use to you. If you put me back in the water, I may grow big and fat, and you can feast on me then."

"That is a tempting idea," Walter said. "But there are no guarantees, little fish. I would be a fool to throw away a good thing I've already got. A little thing in hand is worth more than the hope of a grand thing in the future."

Pandora

adapted by Sarah Marino
illustrated by Charles Kuehn

One day long ago, Zeus, the leader of the gods on Mount Olympus, ordered two brothers to go to earth. Their names were Prometheus and Epimetheus. Zeus told the brothers to create man and animals and to give them strengths to help them survive.

Prometheus set out to create man. He worked patiently and carefully, molding man out of clay and water near a riverbed. Epimetheus, meanwhile, worked in a hurry. He gave the animals great powers, such as skill in hunting, speed, keen eyesight, and, for some, wings to fly. But Epimetheus forgot that man, too, would need special power to survive on earth.

When Prometheus learned that his brother had given the animals the best of the powers, he grew very angry.

"I created man to be a godlike figure," shouted Prometheus. "You have ruined the plan by giving the animals the greatest powers."

"But, brother, perhaps man and animals can share these powers," Epimetheus replied. He bowed his head, ashamed of his mistake.

"Share? As true as that may be, man still needs his own great power…" Prometheus's voice softened as he tried to think of such a power. He sat at the river's edge and looked toward the sun. Several minutes passed. Then Prometheus clasped his hands together. He shouted, "That's it! Man shall gain fire!"

"How will you get fire from Mount Olympus?" asked Epimetheus. "Zeus does not let any but the mightiest gods have the wonders of fire."

"I will find a way," said Prometheus. "To repay me for your mistake, you must stay here and keep man safe until I return. I am going to Mount Olympus."

Epimetheus agreed, and Prometheus disappeared into the sky.

Zeus kept the fire of Mount Olympus burning day and night. The fire was held in a gigantic torch, beside the great golden fountain. Two one-eyed monsters guarded the flame. Prometheus knew he would need help in getting around them. He called on his friend, the wise goddess Athena. With her aid, Prometheus was able to steal a piece of the flame.

Prometheus then returned to his brother on earth. The brothers showed man how to build a fire. Then they taught him how to roast food over the flame.

Soon Zeus could see that man had gained the power of fire. Zeus became angry and decided to punish Prometheus and man. He created a plan and set out to complete it.

First, Zeus told his son Hephaestus to create a woman to go with man. The son created a beautiful mold from the marble of Mount Olympus. He gave the statue the features of the goddesses. Athena blew wit into the statue's ear and made the woman come to life. Aphrodite kissed her cheek and gave her the power of love. The other gods gave her gifts as well, including kindness and feeling. Zeus gave her the gift of unending curiosity. He named her Pandora.

Zeus took Pandora to earth. He presented her as a bride for Epimetheus. Prometheus had told him that Zeus should not be trusted. But Epimetheus did not want to be punished, so he accepted Pandora into his home.

Before Zeus left Pandora, he gave her a small, oddly shaped clay jar with a sealed lid. He told her that it was her duty to protect the jar. He warned her that she should never open it. Pandora agreed, thinking it would be an easy task.

Epimetheus began to adore Pandora's beauty, wit, and kindness. Pandora started to admire her husband as well, and they lived happily, for a time. But Pandora's curiosity would not let her stop thinking of the jar. She carried it with her at all times. Then she realized how much it was taking over her thoughts. She decided to put the jar in the kitchen. It seemed to call to her, though: *Pandora, don't you wonder what I am? Why did Zeus put me in your care? I must be special. Perhaps you could open me and find out?*

Pandora did not know what to do. She tried telling Epimetheus, but he did not understand. He believed that she would obey Zeus.

Finally, after weeks of wondering, Pandora thought, "I suppose it couldn't hurt if I just peek inside." She took the jar and stepped out of the house. She wanted to be in the sunshine and away from her husband. She began to pull on the lid. It loosened easily. She sighed and slowly lifted the lid off of the jar. A great gust of bitterly cold wind blasted out of the jar. Pandora shrieked as it pushed her face. In the stream of wind, she saw many ugly figures emerge and float into the sky: Fear, Jealousy, Anger, Sadness, Gossip, Lies, Blame, Hate—every bad feeling and behavior that man had not yet known. Pandora had just put these bad things onto the earth. Tears began to pour down her face as she tried to put the lid back on the jar. With a great push, she replaced the lid just in time to stop Hope from spilling out. "If Hope had been released, those other awful things would surely have destroyed it," she thought.

Pandora sat down on the ground, holding the jar to her chest with shaking hands. She felt a heavy sadness because of the horrible things that were now in the world. Then, after a few moments, hope crept into her heart. She began to think that it might not be so bad. "As long as we have hope," she thought, "we can fight those evil things and keep happiness alive."

The Concert

written by Summer York

Saturday, August 8, 2015

Dear Diary,

Tonight, I'm going to my first concert ever. I'm really <u>excited</u>! I'm going to see my favorite singer, Taylor Swift.

Last week, my aunt gave me two tickets for my birthday, one for me and one for my cousin, Mia. We were so <u>surprised</u>. Mia and I could not stop squealing! It is the best birthday gift I've ever gotten.

All week I've been <u>pumped</u>…but also <u>frustrated</u>. It felt like the week dragged on endlessly. I thought today would never come. I can't believe the day is FINALLY here.

I'm most <u>eager</u> to hear my favorite Taylor Swift song, "Shake It Off." I like it because the lyrics are fun and the music is upbeat. Mia and I play it over and over while we dance around my room. We're going to scream at the top of our lungs when we hear that song tonight!

It's still kind of early, but I'm going to start getting ready anyway. I'm <u>impatient</u>—I can't sit still for another minute. I'm going to take lots of pictures and paste them on the next few pages. I want to remember this night forever!

Love,

Haley

The High Dive

written by Summer York

July 10th

Dear Journal,

    Today was not a good day. It started off great, but I ended up feeling <u>disappointed</u>. I was <u>thrilled</u> to be meeting my friends at the community pool. There is a big water slide and lots of water cannons, so we always have fun. I was having a blast until Dante wanted to go off the high diving board and everyone agreed. I didn't want to admit that I was <u>nervous</u>. I had never done a dive before, but I went with the group. One by one, my friends dived into the water—Mitchell even did a flip and hit the water stomach first. However, as the line got shorter and my turn loomed, I became increasingly <u>afraid</u>. What if I slipped and got hurt? Worse still, what if I chickened out? I climbed the steep ladder slowly, <u>terrified</u> of the view from the top. I stood there, gripping the handrails, but I couldn't make my feet move forward. Everyone started teasing me, calling me "baby" and "chicken." <u>Hurt</u> and <u>embarrassed</u>, I climbed back down the ladder. I couldn't do it, but now I wish I had tried.

—Justin

Little Red Riding Hood

adapted by Michael Scotto
illustrated by William McCoy III

Once upon a time, many years ago, there lived a very pretty country girl. Her mother loved her. Her grandmother spoiled her even more. Everywhere she went, the pretty girl wore a pretty red hood. The people of her village called her Little Red Riding Hood.

One day, Little Red's mother baked some cakes. She told Little Red, "Take these to Grandmother. She has been very sick. Give her a cake and some butter. And promise me, my lovely girl, that you will stay on the path and not speak to any strangers on your way."

Little Red promised and then left right away. Grandmother lived in the next village over. It was quite a long walk, and the woods got dark early.

Little Red walked and walked through the wood. Soon, she met a wolf. The wolf wanted to eat her right away, but he did not dare. There were woodcutters nearby in the wood. He feared their anger and their axes even more. Instead, the wolf said, "Dear child, what a lovely red hood!"

Little Red was a sweet child. She did not know that wolves are dangerous. His compliment pleased her so much that she forgot her promise to Mother.

"Why, thank you, kind wolf!" she said.

"Where are you off to all by yourself?" asked the wolf.

Little Red smiled and said, "I am going to see my grandmother. I have a cake and some butter to give her from Mother."

"I see," said the wolf, trying to hide his interest. "Is she far away?"

"Oh, she is!" said Little Red. "I have been walking all morning. She is just past the wood, in the first house of the next village."

"Is she, now?" said the wolf, hiding his toothy grin. "Well, I suggest that you take her some flowers with that cake. She will love the flowers that are just off this path. Good luck!"

Little Red thought that was a lovely idea. She left the path to pick some flowers. While she did, the wolf dashed toward Grandmother's house. He arrived in a flash and knocked on the door.

"Who's there?" asked Grandmother.

The wolf raised his voice to sound like a girl. "Your grandchild, with her lovely red hood," he whispered. "I have brought a cake and butter from Mother."

Grandmother, who was in bed, said, "I am still too ill to come to the door, but, please, come in. It is unlocked."

With that, the wolf yanked open the door. He was nearly starved and could not wait. He rushed to Grandmother, and before she could scream, he swallowed her whole. The wolf closed the door. He put on one of Grandmother's nightgowns. Then, he climbed into bed and waited.

Sometime later, the wolf heard a knock at the door.

"Who's there?" asked the wolf, forgetting to change his voice.

Little Red Riding Hood heard the big voice of the wolf and was afraid. But then, she remembered that Grandmother had a cold. Perhaps it had changed her voice.

"It is your grandchild, Little Red Riding Hood," she said. "I have brought a cake and butter from Mother."

The wolf softened his voice as much as he could. "Please, come in," he whispered, pulling on Grandmother's nightcap. "The door is unlocked."

Little Red Riding Hood opened the door.

The wolf hid his body beneath Grandmother's blankets. "Oh, child, I haven't seen you in ages," he whispered. "Put down the cake and butter. Give Grandmother a hug."

Little Red Riding Hood came toward the bed. She noticed that something seemed strange. "Grandmother, what big arms you have!"

"All the better to hug you with, my dear."

"Grandmother," said Little Red, "what big ears you have!"

"All the better to hear you with."

"Grandmother, what big eyes you have!"

"All the better to see you with, my child," said the wolf, smiling a devilish grin.

"Grandmother," said Little Red, "what big teeth you have!"

"All the better to eat you up!"

Little Red let out a scream, and then the wolf ate her up in one bite.

Out in the wood, a woodsman heard Little Red Riding Hood scream. He grabbed his axe and went looking for the sound.

At Grandmother's, the wolf was quite tired. He had not had such a meal in ages. He lay back in bed and fell into a deep, deep sleep.

The woodsman reached Grandmother's house. He saw the open door, went inside, and found the wolf. "I've been looking for you, awful creature," said the woodsman. "You ate the sweet old woman who lives here!"

With this axe, the woodsman cut open the wolf's stomach. His axe was so sharp that it did not wake the wolf. It was a miracle! Grandmother and Little Red were still alive inside. They climbed out carefully and did not wake the wolf. The woodsman and Little Red fetched heavy stones. They filled the wolf's belly with them. They sewed him up with ribbon.

Then, Little Red shouted, "Wake up, wolf!" The wolf woke and tried to flee. But the stones were so heavy that he fell over, dead.

Grandmother shared her cake and butter with the woodsman. "You are a hero, sir," she said.

Meanwhile, Little Red Riding Hood made a promise to herself: "As long as I live, I will never again speak to strangers on the road. I will also stay on the path, like Mother told me."

Twenty Dollars Each

written by Katie Catanzarite

A school bus with broken air conditioning and a bunch of third-graders did not mix particularly well. It was an extremely hot day—unusually hot for early May. Suffice it to say, Jeremy and Aiden could not wait to get home. They knew that Jeremy's mom would have ice cream waiting for them.

The moment the bus lurched to a stop and the bus driver opened the doors, the boys dashed down the steps and jumped onto the sidewalk.

Jeremy's house was just a block away. It was too hot to run, but neither boy wanted to be out in the sun any longer than necessary. Therefore, Jeremy was curious why Aiden stopped in his tracks.

"Come on—it's too hot!" Jeremy whined. "What are you doing?"

"Come here and look at this!"

Aiden bent down and picked something up off the sidewalk. Jeremy reluctantly walked back to his friend to see what he'd found. In Aiden's hands was a brown leather wallet. Aiden flipped it open.

"Whoa!" the boys yelled together.

The wallet was stuffed with twenty-dollar bills. Jeremy snatched the wallet from Aiden and counted the money.

"There's two hundred dollars in here!" he exclaimed. Neither of the boys had held so much money in their lives.

"I could get a new baseball glove," Aiden said.

"I could get a new bike," Jeremy added.

But something wasn't quite right. The boys looked at each other and then down at the wallet again. This time, they noticed the driver's license inside the clear plastic sleeve.

"We can't keep it," Jeremy sighed. He'd already been imagining a shiny new red bike with flames rippling down the sides.

Aiden looked sad too, but the boys knew they had to do the right thing: They had to try to give the wallet back. As soon as they got to Jeremy's house, they told his mom about the wallet. Surprisingly, she knew exactly to whom it belonged—their next-door neighbor, Mr. Jones.

The boys walked with Jeremy's mom next door to Mr. Jones's house. He was out in the front yard, knees in the dirt. He was planting flowers around his mailbox.

The boys' disappointment melted away when they saw the happiness on Mr. Jones's face. He thanked the boys and Jeremy's mom heartily…and then, he removed two twenty-dollar bills and gave them to Jeremy and Aiden.

The boys thanked him enthusiastically and then returned to Jeremy's for that long-awaited ice cream.

The Three Little Pigs

adapted by Ashley Bell
illustrated by Walter Sattazahn

Once upon a time, three little pigs left their parents to explore the world. Through the summer, they traveled, made new friends, and had a lot of fun! They found a town that they loved and decided to call this place their new home. Each pig set out to build a house in this town.

The first little pig, named Percy, wanted to build something quick so that he could continue to play with his friends. He got some straw and built his house in one day. The people in town told him it would never work because straw is not strong enough. He just shrugged his shoulders and went out to play, happy with the house he had built.

Penny, the second pig, thought a house made of straw would be too cold in the winter, so she went out to gather sticks. She spent a few days looking for large sticks. Then, she built her house. She was proud of it, but the townspeople still told her it was not strong enough to last. Not knowing what else to do, she shrugged her shoulders and went out to play with her brother.

The third pig, named Petunia, thought about making her house out of straw or sticks too, but she was not sure that would be the best idea. She remembered something her father had taught her: "Always do your best!" So, she decided to make her house out of bricks, even though it would take her a long time. When she was finally finished, she sat in her new house, proud of the work she had done.

Nearby, a wolf heard that three little pigs had moved into town. He put on a disguise and knocked on Percy's door. He hoped to trick the pig to eat him. But Percy was not fooled. The wolf told him to come

outside, and Percy said, "Not by the hair on my chinny-chin-chin."

The wolf replied, "Then, I'll huff and puff and blow your house in!" The wolf took in a deep breath and blew out. Percy's house of straw fell right over, and Percy ran as fast as he could to Penny's house.

The wolf followed him to Penny's house and knocked on her door. She also was not fooled and refused to let the wolf in. The wolf replied, "Then, I'll huff and puff and blow your house in!" He took another deep breath and blew as hard as he could. Penny's house of sticks fell right over! She and Percy ran quickly to Petunia's house.

The wolf followed them to Petunia's house and tried to trick them one last time. When they would not let him in, he threatened to blow the house down again. He took a deep breath and blew on the house, but, this time, nothing happened. Petunia's house of bricks was strong enough to keep the wolf out. The pigs were all safe. They were all thankful that Petunia had remembered her dad's advice to always do her best!

Theme: "The Boy Who Cried Wolf"

written by Summer York

The popular fable "The Boy Who Cried Wolf" teaches an important lesson. The lesson is that if you lie, no one will believe you when you speak the truth. The boy in the story learns this lesson the hard way. One day, as he is watching the village sheep, he decides to trick the villagers. He cries, "Wolf! Wolf!" All of the villagers come running to help him defend the flock. When they reach the sheep, however, they find that there is no wolf. Instead, the boy had tricked them. After the boy plays the same trick a few more times, the villagers become angry at him for his lies. Then, one evening, a wolf actually threatens the sheep. The boy cries again, "Wolf! Wolf!" Unfortunately, the villagers think that it is just another one of the boy's tricks. No one comes to help him. Because the boy lied about the wolf before, no one believes him when he is telling the truth. As a result, the wolf attacks the flock as the boy watches helplessly. If he had not lied about the wolf before, the villagers would have come and the flock might have been saved.

A Conflict at the Playground

written by Summer York

Priya waved excitedly to Krystal, who stood waiting at the entrance of the playground. With her football tucked under her arm, Priya ran toward her friend.

"Hey!" Priya said in a cheerful greeting. "It's a great day, and we have the whole afternoon!"

Krystal replied, "Yep," but not nearly as enthusiastically. "What do you want to do?"

"I brought my football; we could play catch," Priya suggested, tossing the ball from one hand to the other. Krystal just shrugged and looked bored, so Priya offered, "We can swing on the swings."

- 40 -

"The swings are for babies," Krystal snapped, rolling her eyes. "I'm way too mature for the swings."

"Well," Priya said, looking around, "there are a bunch of kids playing kickball." She gestured toward the field, shading her eyes against the sun. "I can ask them if we can play."

"But they're already in the middle of a game," Krystal pointed out. "They won't want us to interrupt."

"We can at least ask," Priya said. "Maybe they won't care." She was running out of ideas.

"No," Krystal said, folding her arms. "I don't want to play kickball."

"All right," Priya sighed, "what do you want to do?" But Krystal just shrugged again and scuffed the dirt with her sneaker. Priya said, "You must want to do something," trying one last time.

"I don't know," Krystal whined. Exasperated, Priya tossed her football on the ground and sat on it, dropping her head in her hands.

"Krystal," Priya began, "I suggested about a million ideas, and you didn't like any of them. Now it's your turn to suggest something."

"It's not my fault if all of your ideas were lame," Krystal retorted.

At that, Priya had had enough. "Why did you even come to the park?" she asked. Krystal did not respond, so Priya continued. "If you're going to be mean and negative and not want to do anything, I don't think I want to hang out with you."

"Fine, whatever," Krystal retorted, folding her arms.

Finally, Priya yelled, "I'm going home!" She stomped out of the playground, gripping her football tightly.

"Priya, wait!" Krystal called after her. Priya stopped and heard Krystal running to catch up. She grabbed Priya's arm and said, "I'm sorry."

"Why are you being like this?" Priya asked.

Krystal explained. "My parents had a fight. I don't like it when they fight." She wiped away a few tears. "But I didn't mean to take it out on you."

"Krystal," Priya said softly, "why didn't you just tell me?"

"I guess I should have," Krystal admitted. Priya pulled her friend into a hug. "Don't leave. Will you forgive me?"

"It's all right," Priya told her. "Do you want to talk?"

Krystal shook her head. "No. Let's play catch like we planned." Priya held up the football, and Krystal ran for a long pass. Before they knew it, both girls had completely forgotten their disagreement.

Theme: *Little House on the Prairie*

written by Summer York

Laura Ingalls Wilder's *Little House on the Prairie* tells of her family's adventures while traveling through the American West in a covered wagon. One major theme in the book is taking risks to achieve success. In the book, this is known as "pioneer spirit." In the late 1800s, many people made the dangerous journey to settle in the West. Until that time, only Native Americans lived in the Western United States. Brave pioneers, including the Ingalls family, sought a better life in the untamed region. The setting, characters, and plot of Ingalls's book help to support the theme.

The story takes place on the covered wagon trail and in a tiny log house on the prairie. Both settings show the risks that the family took. Traveling in a covered wagon was hazardous. Likewise, living alone on the vast prairie had dangers of its own. On the trail, the Ingalls family has to cross a deep creek. It almost engulfs their wagon. Once they reached their destination, the challenges continue. They have to build a house, hunt for food, build a well for water, and store provisions for the winter. However, through all of these dangers, Pa feels that the risk is worth the reward of gaining good farmland.

The characters in the story (Pa, Ma, Mary, Laura, and Carrie) are brave and strong. Pa has the pioneer spirit. He moves his family westward to claim a good plot of land. The trek is dangerous, but Pa is capable of protecting his wife and daughters. He knows how to navigate the trail. He is a good hunter, builder, and farmer. Pa also sings and plays the fiddle. He makes his family laugh to keep up their spirits. The family works together to make a comfortable life on the wild prairie.

The plot of this story involves daily risk to the lives of the family members. Pa sells the house in the big woods of Wisconsin and moves the family West in a covered wagon. Prairie life is not easy, though. The Ingalls family faces many dangers. The entire family catches a fever. They are only cured with the help of their distant neighbors. One night, a pack of menacing wolves surrounds their tiny house. They even have to fight a raging prairie fire that threatens their home.

The setting, characters, and plot of this novel contribute to its theme. The Ingalls family faced many risks in the name of building a better life for themselves on the prairie.

Works Cited

Wilder, Laura Ingalls. *Little House on the Prairie*. Harper & Brothers, 1935.

The Librarian

written by Katie Catanzarite

Jill and Andrew stood on the steps of the Springfield Public Library, too afraid to go inside. They were too afraid even to peek through the glass doors. Their third grade teacher, Mrs. Tanner, had assigned them a history project. They had to choose any public figure that significantly impacted America's past and write a report about that figure. There was one catch, though: Mrs. Tanner also wanted them to go to the library and have Mr. Rossini help them choose their public figure.

Jill and Andrew had never met Mr. Rossini, the school librarian. They'd heard stories from the sixth graders on the playground, though. Mr. Rossini was an old, mean man with a hunched back and a glass eye that never closed. He could see and watch you even in his sleep. Mrs. Tanner had assured her students that Mr. Rossini was a perfectly nice man, but Jill and Andrew were still unsure.

"Let's just get it over with," Andrew said. "We'll just choose…Abraham Lincoln. We just need to find the L books, check out the first book we find, and get out."

Jill agreed. The two of them ran up the steps and pushed open the heavy glass door. A worn, brass bell clanged above their heads, making them both jump. Inside, the library smelled sour and musty—like

— 43 —

nobody had been there in years. There was no sign of Mr. Rossini.

"Come on, this way," Andrew said. He led Jill to the closest shelf.

"You check that end, I'll check—" Andrew froze in terror as he came face to face with Mr. Rossini. He really did have a hunched back! His skin was yellow and leathery. Thin white hair stuck out of his head in all directions.

"Can I help you find anything?" he asked. His voice was slightly raspy, but surprisingly soft.

"Um…" Andrew stammered. "We were just… looking…we have a history report…." His voice trailed off and he backed up, smacking into Jill.

Jill stepped forward and demanded, "Do you really have a glass eye?"

Mr. Rossini's face split into a wide grin and he howled with laughter. He leaned against the bookshelf for support and shook his head.

"Is that what they're saying about me now?" he asked between bouts of chuckling.

"So you don't, then?" Jill seemed a little disappointed. Mr. Rossini calmed down and smiled at her.

"I'm afraid not, but I do have a titanium knee."

"You do?" Andrew exclaimed. "That's awesome!"

Mr. Rossini laughed again. "Now, what are you kids really looking for?"

"We have a report due on any famous historical figure," Jill said. "We were going to pick Abraham Lincoln."

Mr. Rossini paused and considered that for a moment. "Abraham Lincoln is a great choice," he said. "But, I guarantee three other groups will report on him as well…. Say, have either of you heard of Helen Keller?"

Gum, Now and Then

written by Bryon Gill
illustrated by William McCoy III

Wyatt knew better than to take the gum, but it was his favorite kind, and he wanted it very badly. He looked down the aisle, where his sister was counting soup cans and his mother was trying to find the low-sodium green beans.

"Why do they all have so much *salt*?" his mother said to no one in particular.

Wyatt looked once—and then once more—at the cashier, who was busy with her cell phone. He listened to the song playing on the old radio that was sitting next to the register; it was playing some old love song that his mother would probably sing along to under her breath. Wyatt reached out to grab the small yellow package, but he then pulled his hand back, uncertain.

He almost didn't go through with it, but then his sister knocked over a soup can, and somehow that made his arm just *go*. He reached out, grabbed the gum, and slipped it in his coat pocket.

The gum burned a hole in Wyatt's pocket the whole way home. He wanted to take it out and chew a stick, but how would he explain it? Then, it occurred to him: There was no way he was going to get away with his crime. He was so excited about the gum—but even more nervous about what would happen when he was discovered. *Maybe I should just chew some now*, he thought. *If I get caught, I won't get any.* He knew that his sister would smell it, though, in the seat right next to him. She'd probably want some, and then she'd have a secret, and Little-Miss-Perfect was good at everything but keeping secrets. *No*, he thought, *I should get rid of it.* How could he do that, though? Wyatt knew that he couldn't eat it all; it would stick in his stomach for eight years (according to his friend Brandon), and he'd still have the wrappers to dispose of. Could he hide it under the front seat of the car? His sister would see that for sure. Finally, Wyatt decided to throw the stolen gum out the window; he pressed a button, and the window started to roll down.

Wyatt's mother yelled before he could get it down far enough to fit more than a gum stick. "Wyatt! What are you doing? I thought I had the child lock set on that, and it's twelve degrees outside!"

He rolled the window back up and then put his hand back in his pocket, clutching the gum tight.

"What are you thinking?" his mother asked. "If you're hot, just tell me and I'll adjust the climate controls."

Wyatt put his head down and muttered under his breath, "Sorry, it was an accident."

"How do you accidentally roll down a window?" his mother asked, but she let it go at that.

The drive home was long because of traffic, but the family eventually got home. Wyatt hung up his coat without thinking about what was in his pockets. Wyatt's mother asked him where his gloves were. Wyatt knew that they were in his hat, but his mother was already checking his coat pockets for them. She pulled the shiny package of gum out.

"What's this?" she asked. "Wyatt! Come here this instant!"

Wyatt shuffled over to his mother, already close to tears.

"Where did you get this?"

Wyatt put his hands in his pockets. "I don't know," he mumbled.

"You expect me to believe that you don't know how a pack of gum made its way into your coat pocket? I'm going to give you one more chance to be honest with me. Where did you get this?"

"Am I going to be in trouble?" Wyatt asked.

"You are already in trouble," his mother said, "and now you'd better be honest with me. Did you get into the Easter candy and take this?"

Relief flooded through Wyatt. "Yes," he lied. "I'm sorry, Mom. I won't do it again."

His mother met his gaze firmly and said, "It's important to be honest. When we lie to people, even about little things, they eventually find out, and then they don't trust you when it's important. I'm not going to ground you this time since you owned up to what you did. I'm going to put this back now."

As Wyatt's mother turned to return the gum to the Easter stash, Wyatt tried to ask her to wait—to explain what he really did—but his mouth felt like it was full of sand. He couldn't make himself say the words. When Wyatt's mother reached her bedroom closet, he could feel a change in the air. She slammed the door and returned to him.

"I am very disappointed in you, Wyatt. Tell me the truth now—did you steal this?" In her left hand, Wyatt's mother held the pack of gum he stole, and in her right, she held an unopened ten-pack of gum.

"Don't even talk; I don't want to hear another story," she said before Wyatt could answer. "We are going back to the store right now. We're returning *both* of these, and you're going to apologize to the owner. You're grounded for a month."

Easter was in a month, Wyatt realized with sadness, and there would be no gum, then or now.

— 46 —

The Runt Horse

written by Sarah Marino
illustrated by Dion Williams

In a time long before this one, herds of mustangs roamed freely along the coast of the Atlantic Ocean. One particular herd roamed on an island, and in this herd, there was a runt of a horse named Ruby. She was teased continuously by the other horses: "Runty Ruby, you're no good. We should send you to the waves. You're fish food." Her mama and papa would never participate in the teasing, but sometimes they would look ashamed, lowering their heads as they made their way through the terrain with Ruby.

From the time she was young, Ruby wanted to be separate from the herd and explore the place beyond their island. As a runt, she felt like she didn't belong. She had made the mistake of making this dream known in front of Alex, the teenage horse whose bullying was the worst, and he had taunted her about it since. "You'll never make it out of here," he would say. "You would never survive. Another herd would come along and maul you, if a seagull didn't get you first!" He would laugh at his own bullying words, and then he'd continue, "Not me, though. I'm getting out soon. I'll explore and become king of another herd." As much as she considered him an enemy, Ruby was thankful she wasn't the only one who dreamed of exploring.

***

If Ruby was a runt, she was a pretty one, though. Her sleek black fur was so dark and shiny that in the sunlight, it shone a purplish color. She was smart, too, and even impressed the wise old horses who could barely trot anymore and only stood all day, talking about the time before and giving advice. One day Ruby had come walking up to a group of them by herself as they talked in hushed voices.

"Ah, Ruby, the little mare. What can we do for you?" said Xavier, the spotted old horse.

"I'm just wandering. Alex was picking on me again. He said all of the horses want me to leave," Ruby said.

"Ruby," said Xavier, "do you know why we were speaking so quietly just now?"

Ruby shook her head.

"There is some trouble beyond our coast. We cannot name it at this time. But we fear that horses like Alex will do us harm. The trouble could be serious. We might need your help," Xavier explained.

"I will try to help in any way I can," said Ruby.

"We thought so," said another wise old horse, Gertrude. "You are an important ally, Ruby. Please

don't forget us. And don't mention to anyone what we've discussed."

Ruby nodded. She thought it odd that Gertrude asked her not to forget them (how could she ever?), but she smiled and didn't reply.

The old horses put their heads down and began to walk toward the ocean, a glowing silver serpent in the distance. Ruby knew this was their signal to her that the conversation had ended and she should be on her way. She turned and trotted toward the waves in the opposite direction.

***

A few days later, Ruby was galloping along the water's edge as the sun rose. The waves were music to her ears, and she kept time with them in her steps. The sun was a fiery orange pool of light just brightening the horizon over the water. Pink and purple clouds floated above. Ruby was mesmerized, so much so that she failed to see Alex running toward her.

"Ruby, my little friend. How did I guess you'd be here?" he whinnied and smiled slyly.

"Because I do this every day, maybe?" Ruby said.

"Listen, I have a plan. The herd is still asleep. We could leave, now." His beady black eyes were blinking rapidly. He stared at her, digging his two front hoofs into the sand.

"What are you talking about? Where would we go? And why would I go anywhere with you?" Ruby asked.

"So many questions. Follow me, and your questions will be answered." Alex started trotting toward a dune ten yards away. Ruby followed reluctantly.

At the top of the dune, she saw what he meant. It looked like the towns from the time before that she'd heard the wise old horses talking about—from the time before the great flood. And there! Ruby couldn't stop herself from neighing. "People!" she cried.

— 48 —

"That's right! I'm going to work for them. I'll get to explore and get off of this island!" Alex pranced excitedly like a colt after it's learned it can walk.

"You're wrong. They'll make you work for nothing. They'll keep you in a pen," Ruby said. "Don't you ever listen?" She snorted angrily at him.

"I've been watching them, Runty. They already have horses. See? Over there."

"But we're different. We roam on this land. We are wild. It's not the life for us, Alex."

"You don't get it. I'm going to be free and see the world! Too bad you're a runt and they wouldn't take you anyway." He began trotting toward the tents and people. Ruby followed but stayed close to the dune weeds. She tried to keep herself hidden.

Alex galloped right up to a man and woman standing near an area where some horses were grazing. There was a fence around these horses. They were big and looked tougher than any horses Ruby had ever seen.

The woman saw Alex and jumped behind the man. "How did he get out?" she asked.

"Hmm, I don't think that's one of ours," the man said. He took a long look at Alex, walking around him several times.

Alex whinnied and shook his mane. He shouted to Ruby, "See? I'll be fed and turn plump like these fellows." Sure enough, the woman brought around a bucket of carrots and apples. Alex squealed like a pig, taking large bites of everything.

Eventually, the woman noticed Ruby and alerted the man.

"Now that's strange," he said, looking at Ruby. "That's a runt horse, for sure."

Ruby suddenly had an idea. She began to droop her head and shake slightly, bending one leg as if she were hobbled. She tried to drool a bit, hoping that if she looked quite bad, the people wouldn't want her or the rest of the herd.

"I was going to go and see if these two came from a herd. We could use some others," the man said. "But they could be fit for nothing, like this runt. Nah, we'll just keep this boy. He's a machine; I can tell."

"I've got the harness ready," the woman said a few minutes later.

"Steady, steady there," the man said, petting Alex's back.

The woman threw the harness over Alex. The man grabbed it and began pulling Alex toward the pen. Alex was still chewing as he realized what was happening. He began to neigh and shake his head roughly. The man pulled harder. Ruby could take no more. She ran away, still trying to look hobbled, and then bolted after she was beyond the dune. She realized now what the wise old horses had meant.

Despite the awful teasing Alex had put her through, Ruby felt sorry for him. She ran to the old horses to tell them what she had seen. They seemed to already know. Gertrude nuzzled Ruby gently and told her she had done a good thing.

"But, Alex," Ruby began.

"Alex made his own choices," Xavier said. "We all must face the consequences of our actions. It is good to explore, but we are wild horses. That is a very different life from what we've known. You must know what you are Ruby, and you must love what you are."

From that day on, no one teased Ruby and she didn't mind being a runt. She knew she had made a difference, and when the time came, she took her place among the wise old horses.

– 49 –

Popcorn Explosion Causes Kernel Chaos in Local Neighborhood

written by Summer York
illustrated by Dion Williams

ORVILLE COUNTY – Neighbors had a huge mess to clean up following an explosion at the Poplar Popcorn Factory in Kettle Township. On Tuesday afternoon, the popping machine overflowed, causing two tons of popcorn to spill through the windows of the factory and out into the streets.

Mr. Stan Poplar, 54, and his wife Jan Poplar, 50, own the factory. They said the explosion happened because they were arguing about how many popcorn kernels to pop.

"I thought we had enough," Mrs. Poplar said. "But Mr. Poplar thought we should make more than usual."

Mr. Poplar explained that the kernels are stored inside a huge vat. The vat is connected by a chute to the popping machine. The chute is opened to drop kernels into the popping machine and closed when there are enough.

"But we were so busy arguing," Mrs. Poplar said, "that neither of us closed the chute. We didn't notice that the kernels were still spilling into the machine."

"The popping machine is not supposed to hold such a large load," Mr. Poplar said. "We produce about two tons of popcorn in a month, and we had just dumped that same amount in all at once. We didn't know what was going to happen."

One witness, a hair stylist who was working at Sally's Salon across the street, said she could hear loud popping noises coming from the factory.

"The noises started around 1:00 p.m. on Tuesday," she said. "We all ran outside to see where the noises were coming from. Then we saw popcorn flowing out of the factory windows!" She described the scene as frantic.

"People were running out of their homes and businesses to see all the fuss," she said. "Traffic had to stop because the popcorn was blocking the roads. Some people even started eating the popcorn right off the ground."

Mrs. Poplar said that inside the factory it was just as chaotic. She said that in the commotion, she tried to remember how to turn the machine off.

"But Mr. Poplar kept yelling and running around in a panic," she said. "I couldn't even hear myself think!"

When the popcorn started spilling out of the machine and filling the floor around them, the Poplars knew they needed help.

"Nothing like this had ever happened before," Mr. Poplar said. "We didn't know what to do."

That was when the factory foreman, 35-year-old Joe Smith, ran into the room. "Luckily for us," Mrs. Poplar said, "Joe knew exactly what to do."

"We have emergency drills here at the factory about once a month," Smith explained. "So everyone knows what to do when something like this happens."

But Smith, who has been the factory foreman for eight years, said that the Poplars never practiced the emergency drills with the rest of the factory workers. "They were in a panic when I came into the room," Smith said. "There was popcorn everywhere, and it was still popping. So I told them we all needed to get out of the factory and call 911."

Chief Terrence D. Higgins, head of the Kettle Township Police Department, was among the first on the scene.

"In all my years as a law officer, I've never seen anything like this," he stated. "It is a good thing that no one was hurt."

He also said the Poplars were fortunate that their workers practiced regular emergency drills.

"We have found that practicing for an emergency helps you to be more prepared when the real thing happens," Higgins said. He pointed out three things that everyone should remember. "First, you should remain calm. Second, you should protect yourself by getting away from a dangerous situation. Third, you should call for help immediately."

"Our emergency drills definitely helped me to know what to do," Smith said. "I hope now Mr. and Mrs. Poplar will practice with us."

The Poplars said they have definitely learned their lesson.

"We realize now that we should have practiced the emergency drills so that we would have known what to do," Mrs. Poplar said.

"We did everything wrong," Mr. Poplar agreed. "We should have stayed calm, left the building immediately, and called for help. We should not have stood there arguing."

Chief Higgins said that despite the mess, there was no real damage to the factory. Now Kettle Township residents just have to figure out how to clean up all the popcorn. The manager of the local grocery store was helping with the cleanup effort.

"I've been bagging the popcorn and selling it in my store," he said. "Lots of people have been out here with brooms. The kids are eating as much as they can. Even the birds are helping to eat the popcorn."

The owner of Cinema World, the local movie theater, also agreed to help out. He has been handing out free popcorn to all moviegoers.

"It has been great for my business," he said. "I've sold almost twice as many tickets as usual!"

Kettle Township Mayor William Jones is offering residents of surrounding towns free popcorn for the entire week if they are willing to help with the cleanup.

"All in all," the mayor said, "this hasn't been a total disaster. The entire community is working together. The factory wasn't damaged, and Mr. Poplar has since 'buttered' things over with his wife."

The Poplars said that they will continue popcorn production as soon as the mess is cleaned up. The factory, located at the corner of Canola Street and Lincoln Avenue, was originally built in 1968. It was originally a jelly bean factory that was run by Mrs. Kelly Green. The Poplars bought the factory in 2000 and turned it into the Poplar Popcorn Factory. The factory currently produces about two tons of popcorn per month, or 24 tons a year. It is the largest popcorn factory in Orville County.

A Swing Set Story

written by Vincent J. Scotto

Harold hadn't always been a confident boy. He was regularly picked last to play games at the park; often, he didn't even try to join in. He usually went to the swings. At least there he didn't have to compete with anyone. Harold didn't mind playing alone, but things were about to change.

One hot evening in July, Harold went to the park as usual. Some of the neighborhood kids were already playing kickball, so he went directly for the swing set.

Something was different, though. Someone was already there, swinging away. When Harold got close, he could see that it was the sort of person who frightened him the most. It was a girl.

"I'm Genesis," she said confidently. "What's your name?"

"Are you talking to me?" Harold asked as he began to swing higher.

"Who else would I be talking to if you're the only one around?"

"I'm Harold," he said timidly. "Did you just move here?"

"Yeah. I was going to play with the other kids, but I don't really know anyone yet."

"That's all right," Harold said. "I don't play with them much either. I prefer swinging."

Genesis giggled. "I guess we can be loners together!" she proclaimed. "What do you think?"

"Sounds good to me," Harold said as he smiled.

The two kids met at the park every day to swing on the swing set. They spent each afternoon laughing and soaring. They talked about their families, shared secrets, and challenged each other to swinging contests. They soon became great friends. Harold couldn't have been happier, but something was about to mess everything up.

One day, when Harold had plans to meet Genesis, he was running a bit late. He had to clean his room before his grandmother would let him go to the park. By the time Harold arrived, he found that Genesis was already there on the swings. This time, though, she was with another boy. The new boy, Bryan, had moved to town in September. Harold didn't really know him, but Bryan was much bigger, and that scared Harold a bit.

Harold had never dared to approach him, but now he'd have to if he wanted to swing with Genesis.

"Hey, Gen," Harold said softly.

"Harold, where have you been?" she asked. "I was waiting for a bit, but then Bryan came over."

Bryan stopped swinging and said, "What's up, dude?"

Harold winced at Bryan and turned to Genesis. "I thought we were swinging today."

"You snooze, you lose, dude!" Bryan laughed.

"We can all hang out," Genesis insisted. "Right, Bryan?"

"There's only two swings!" Bryan said. "You're just going to have to find something else to do."

"Genesis and I always swing," Harold said in a shaky voice. Bryan got off the swing and came very close to Harold. Bryan stood tall and looked down at him.

"I said beat it, dude."

Bryan shoved Harold to the ground. Harold hit it hard and tears welled up in his eyes.

"Ha, are you gonna cry now?" Bryan teased.

Harold shuffled to his feet and ran away.

Joel's Birthday

written by Jennifer Tkocs

This was going to be the worst birthday ever.

Normally, on my birthday, my parents wake me up bright and early for a special breakfast. My mom makes these great pancakes shaped like bears, and we all eat together at the kitchen table. She only does that for my birthday. I thought for sure there would be bear pancakes waiting for me when I woke up.

But there were no bear pancakes to be found in the kitchen this morning. My parents were both sitting at the table, reading the paper.

"Good morning, Joel," my dad said. That was it—no mention of my birthday at all.

I tried to brush it off. I made myself a bowl of cereal and ate it in silence. I had expected that a friend would have called by now. That's what happens on birthdays—your friends call. But the phone was not ringing.

After breakfast, I decided to go outside for a walk. Maybe my friends were waiting at the tire swing in my backyard. I laced up my sneakers and walked outside. Two of my friends lived just down the street. They loved our tire swing. Sometimes, they would come over and swing on it even if I wasn't home. But today, the tire was swinging in the wind all by itself.

I wondered if my friends could be at the playground. It was nice weather, and it was Saturday. We always had fun at the playground, swinging on the monkey bars and trying to run up the slides without slipping. Surely someone had to be there. I walked the few blocks to the end of our neighborhood. There were always a few people I knew at the playground. Today, however, all the slides and swings were empty.

This never happens! I thought. I could always find someone to hang out with. I didn't want to spend the whole day by myself. After all, it was my birthday.

There was one place left to check. Maybe my friends had decided to go to the baseball field and play a pickup game. Some of the best afternoons I'd ever had were spent right on that little diamond. Usually someone would call and invite me if there was a game, but maybe they just forgot. I walked back to my house and grabbed my baseball glove, just in case. Then, I got on my bike and rode all the way to the ball field.

The ball field was packed, but it was just a kindergarten tee-ball game. None of my friends would be caught dead hanging out there.

I checked my watch. It was almost noon. No one had called me. My friends were nowhere to be found. My parents hadn't even remembered that it was my birthday. This was the worst birthday ever.

I rode my bike to the little convenience store down the road from the baseball field. My friends and I loved the donuts they sold there. Since everyone forgot my birthday, I decided to buy myself a birthday treat. I used all of my allowance money to buy four cream-stuffed donuts. I ate them on the ride home.

I was so bummed out that I wanted to just go straight to bed. I opened the door to the house, prepared to walk right past my parents and up to my room.

However, as I opened the door, a balloon floated right into my head. "Happy Birthday!" it said. My parents had remembered after all!

I walked toward the kitchen, hoping that maybe my bear-shaped pancakes would be there after all. Instead of pancakes, though, I saw nine familiar faces.

"HAPPY BIRTHDAY, JOEL!" my friends shouted.

They had remembered! All of them! "Man," I said, "you guys really got me!" This was going to be the BEST birthday ever.

Jake and Jake

written by Mark Weimer

Everyone is different. Each person comes from a different family and has different hobbies. Every now and then, you might meet someone who just does not seem to fit in. Have you ever been at the playground and noticed someone who was not playing with anyone else? Most often, it is not because these people do not want to play. Rather, they might be shy, or they might simply be waiting for someone to invite them. Who knows? The next time you see a lonely kid, extend an invitation to play. You might just find a new best friend. It is not always easy, but that is how I found my best friend.

One day, my friends and I were playing football **during** school recess. Recess was **between** math and lunch. I was a star athlete on my peewee football team, so, **at first**, I was just focused on scoring touchdowns. **During** the game, I rarely looked around to see what everyone else was doing. **After** a while, however, touchdowns became boring, and I **eventually** started to look around.

Before recess ended, I noticed the new boy in our class. He was sitting alone on a bench. He was dragging his foot along the ground and appeared as though he was bored. **As soon as** I scored one last touchdown, I decided to walk over and introduce myself. **In the meantime**, everybody stopped playing football and watched. I **suddenly** noticed that all eyes were on me. **After** what felt like a long walk, I finally reached the boy and introduced myself. "Hi, my name is Jake." **As soon as** I said "Jake," the new boy's head snapped up.

"Jake?" he asked. "That's my name, too! We have the same name!" **Before** he could say anything else, I sat down beside him.

"You're new here. Would you like to come play football with us?" I asked.

"Yes!" he said **immediately**. "I hoped somebody would come and ask." **Shortly after that**, we were both playing football with the rest of our classmates. It was the first time I had seen Jake smile since he was in school. When recess was over, it was time for lunch. I invited him to sit with my friends, and they all thought that one Jake was as cool as the other Jake. From then on, we were always together. We could not have met each other sooner, and we became best friends.

Many kids find themselves lost when they move to a new school. They do not know anybody, and sometimes, it is really hard for them to fit in. That is why it is very important to help them. You never know if you yourself may have to move someday. You may find yourself in an unfamiliar school with new people. The sooner you start to make friends, the more fun school can be. There is no such thing as having too many friends. Besides, you never know who may become one of your best friends.

King Midas and the Golden Touch

written by Debbie Parrish
illustrated by David Rushbrook

Long, long ago, there lived a king named Midas. Midas was a good king with many fine qualities. He loved to have fun. He especially enjoyed his beautiful rose garden. Midas spent hours walking through the garden, enjoying the sweet smells and the beauty of the flowers. His best quality, though, was that he was a good and loving father. He often had fun picking his freshest roses and making a bouquet for his beloved daughter.

But Midas had one flaw, one weakness in his character. He often made decisions quickly, without thinking about what the outcome might be. He did not stop to think about the consequences of his actions.

One day, King Midas was looking over all of his wonderful treasures when he had a surprise visitor. The god Dionysus appeared to him. Dionysus told Midas that he was going to reward him for being a good king. The god offered to grant Midas any one wish that he wanted to make. Of course, Midas did not stop to think. He immediately blurted out the first wish that came to mind.

"I wish that everything I touch will turn to gold!" shouted Midas. "That way, I will never want for anything."

Dionysus warned the king to think long and hard about his wish. "Be very sure, Midas."

"I am sure," replied Midas. "My mind is made up. There is no use wasting time thinking about it any longer!"

As he had promised, Dionysus granted King Midas's wish. Midas was pleased with his good fortune. He decided to take a walk in his garden. Midas always found that to be a pleasant way to spend his afternoon.

In the garden, Midas happily decided that he would try out his new powers. Seeing a stone in his path, Midas leaned over to pick it up. Immediately the stone turned to gold. The great king was so pleased that he quickly reached down and plucked a blade of grass from between the bushes. The grass also magically turned to gold. Midas's excitement grew!

A smiling King Midas walked around his garden, all the while thinking, "I will be the richest of all men."

Midas stopped to pick one of his roses, and, once again, his touch turned the flower to gold. Hardly able to believe his good luck, Midas admired a lovely nightingale as it fluttered around his garden. As he usually did, Midas held out his finger for the bird to fly down and perch. The moment the bird grazed his finger, Midas saw it turn to gold and drop heavily to the ground.

All of this was getting a bit overwhelming for the king. He was getting hungry as well. He decided to go inside and have his daily feast.

Midas sat down to enjoy a huge loaf of crusty bread. Hungrily he reached for the bread only to find that as soon as he touched it, the bread turned to gold. The king became irritated. He began to think for the first time that he may have made a mistake with his

wish. Midas grew thirsty and reached for a cup to take a refreshing drink. That, too, became a solid piece of gold.

A hungry, thirsty, and confused Midas called for his dear daughter to come and comfort him. The very sight of her made him feel better. Midas walked over to his daughter and took her into his arms. The moment that she put her arms around her father, the girl turned to a shiny gold statue. When Midas felt the cold, hard statue in his arms, his heart was broken. The person he loved most in the world was taken from him.

Now Midas was sorry that he had ever made his wish. He did not realize what a mistake he had made until he lost the very thing that meant the most to him. King Midas went to Dionysus and begged him to take away his power.

"Are you sure that this is what you want?" asked Dionysus.

"I am absolutely sure!" replied Midas.

"That is what you said last time," Dionysus reminded him.

"Now I have thought about it long and hard. I may lose all of my riches and everything may turn to dust, but those things are no longer important to me."

Dionysus told Midas, "Very well, then. You must go to the Pactolus River and wash in its waters."

Midas hurried to the river. As he washed himself, gold flowed from Midas into the water. From the water the gold settled into the sand.

Midas was very relieved to have lost his golden touch that day. He promised himself that he would no longer be so quick to make decisions. He would think about the consequences of his actions. From then on, whenever Midas needed time to think, he would take a long walk along the banks of the Pactolus River. Even today, the sand there remains a special golden color.

Book Report: *Charlie and the Chocolate Factory*

written by Luke See

Charlie and the Chocolate Factory was written in 1964. Roald Dahl wrote this book. Dahl wrote many popular books for children. *Charlie and the Chocolate Factory* might be his most famous book.

This book is set in England. It tells a story about the world's greatest chocolate factory. A man named Mr. Willy Wonka owns the factory. In the book, Willy Wonka opens his factory to the public for the first time in many years. People all around the world are very excited. Willy Wonka hides five golden tickets inside the wrappers of his chocolate bars. Each person who finds a ticket is invited to visit his factory.

In addition to Willy Wonka, the children who find the golden tickets are the important characters in the book. Augustus Gloop, Veruca Salt, Violet Beauregarde, and Mike Teavee all find golden tickets. The fifth character to find a golden ticket is Charlie Bucket. He is the main character of the story. Charlie comes from a very poor family. He finds the last golden ticket. Charlie's Grandpa Joe travels to the factory with Charlie. He is another important character. The story follows the children as they journey through the factory. The children quickly learn that if they misbehave, they are ejected from the factory in painful ways.

Works Cited

Dahl, Roald. *Charlie and the Chocolate Factory*. Alfred Knopf, 1964.

Book Report: *Matilda*

written by Luke See

Author Roald Dahl wrote *Matilda* in 1988. Dahl is famous for many other children's stories, such as *James and the Giant Peach* and *Charlie and the Chocolate Factory*. *Matilda* is named for its main character, a very smart young girl named Matilda. The action is set in England. The city where the story takes place is not named. Many scenes take place at Matilda's house and her school.

Matilda has several important supporting characters. Matilda's parents, the Wormwoods, pay little attention to her. Miss Jennifer Honey is Matilda's teacher. Miss Honey is very kind to Matilda. She treats Matilda as if the girl were her own beloved daughter. Matilda has a good friend named Lavender. Finally, there is the headmistress of the school, Agatha Trunchbull. Miss Trunchbull is the villain of the story. She terrorizes the students at her school.

In addition to being very smart, Matilda possesses certain special powers. One of these is telekinesis. This power allows Matilda to move objects with her mind. Matilda uses her special powers to help her new friends. She fights to rid the school of the frightening Miss Trunchbull. This book became so popular that it was made into a movie and a famous musical.

Works Cited

Dahl, Roald, and Quentin Blake. *Matilda*. Viking Kestrel, 1988.

Book Report: *Stuart Little*

written by Luke See
illustrated by Walter Sattazahn

E. B. White is the author of the book *Stuart Little*. He wrote it in 1945. Today, 60 years later, it is a classic and still a favorite among people everywhere. This book is named for its main character, Stuart Little. Stuart is a small, mouse-like boy who is born to a family of regular-sized people. When he is born, the doctor describes him as having "a mouse's sharp nose, a mouse's tail, and a mouse's whiskers, and the pleasant shy manner of a mouse."

Despite Stuart's unusual appearance, his parents raise him as if he were no different from any other boy. Stuart has two parents and an older brother, George. Stuart also spends time with some other animals. These include Snowbell, the family cat, and Margalo, a pet bird. Snowbell the cat often bothers Stuart. Margalo the bird, however, becomes his good friend.

The story is mainly set in New York City. It follows Stuart's life from his birth until he becomes an adult. Stuart has many adventures in New York City during his youth. He uses his unique size to his advantage. He races model sailboats and cars in Central Park. Soon, Stuart's journey takes him across the country. Throughout the story, he experiences life just a little differently from everyone else.

Works Cited

White, E. B., and Garth Williams. *Stuart Little*. Harper & Brothers, 1945.

Book Report: *The Velveteen Rabbit*

written by Luke See

The Velveteen Rabbit was written in 1922. The author of this book is Margery Williams. *The Velveteen Rabbit* tells the story of a stuffed rabbit sewn from velveteen. Velveteen is a type of fabric. The rabbit is given to a small boy as a Christmas present. The story follows the rabbit's existence.

This book is not really set in a specific country or city. Instead, it takes place mainly in two locations. Much of the story occurs in a nursery. The rabbit is either locked away there or left on the floor. The story also takes place in the woods near the boy's home.

The characters, like the setting, are also unnamed. Except for the rabbit, most of the characters are just identified by their descriptions. Characters include "the boy" and other people, such as "the boy's nana" and "the doctor." The only other character with a name is the Skin Horse. He is an old and wise toy horse. He is very important to the story. Early on, the Skin Horse tells the rabbit that if he is loved enough by a child, he can become real. The rabbit's driving wish is to become real. The story follows the rabbit's quest to not only be loved by his owner, but to become real because of that love. This quest finally takes the rabbit into the woods, where he meets a magical fairy. The fairy kisses him, and he becomes real.

Works Cited

Bianco, Margery Williams, and Michael Hague. *The Velveteen Rabbit, Or, How Toys Become Real*. Holt, Rinehart and Winston, 1983.

TAM, TAM, the Answer Man

written by Debbie Parrish
illustrated by David Rushbrook

Long, long ago, just outside of a small village, lay a thickly grown forest. Through the forest was a long walking path. Many people liked to take a stroll along this path when they had a problem they needed to resolve. It was well known by the townspeople that a tiny man with a very strong voice lived in the forest. The first ones to meet him had named him the Answer Man. Ever since, when a person had a problem that lay heavily on his mind, he would spend some time walking the path and then call out for the Answer Man. Everyone who truly desired help always seemed to leave with good advice. Over time, those he had helped gave the Answer Man a friendly nickname: TAM.

Villagers of all ages sought the help of TAM. One day, a little boy was feeling very frightened. He had broken his mother's favorite bowl and was afraid about telling her. The boy did not know what to do. He feared getting in trouble with his parents. He didn't want to be punished and maybe miss going to his friend's house that week.

The boy decided to take a walk on the path and speak with TAM about it. Entering the forest, the little boy called out, "TAM, TAM, the Answer Man, solve my problem, if you can!" TAM appeared and asked the boy why he was troubled. The boy explained his problem, and TAM began to talk with him about his feelings. TAM asked the boy how his mother would feel not knowing what happened to her bowl. He asked the boy how it made him feel inside to keep the accident to himself.

Then TAM advised the boy, "Keeping the truth inside of you will only bring you misery. And if anyone learns that you hid the truth, you will be known as someone who cannot be trusted to do what is right. Go to your mother and tell her what you did. You will feel better and your mother will respect your honesty." Then, as suddenly as he appeared, TAM was nowhere to be seen.

Another time, a teenage girl came to visit TAM. She had just left a group of her girlfriends. They had been teasing a younger girl by making fun of her clothes and telling her that she was ugly. The teenage girl had joined in with her friends because it seemed like the thing to do. She wanted to be accepted as part of the group, didn't she? But, the closer she got to the forest, the worse she felt about what she had done. "TAM, TAM, the Answer Man, solve my problem, if you can!" called the girl. TAM appeared almost immediately.

"Do you want to be accepted, or do you want to do what is right?" TAM asked the girl. "Sometimes doing the right thing is hard, but it feels much better than doing something unkind. Go to the young girl and apologize. Then, if this happens again, do not join in with the crowd. Do what is right!" And then, poof, TAM was gone.

On another day, it was an old man who felt the need to talk to TAM. The man lived with his son's family. His wife was dead, and he did not feel that his family needed him anymore. As he entered the forest, the old man said in a sad voice, "TAM, TAM, the Answer Man, solve my problem, if you can."

Of course, TAM came right out to talk with the old man. TAM listened as the old man told him how lonely he felt and how no one in his family needed him anymore. "Well, who said you can only be needed by your family?" asked TAM. "There are many people in the world who need someone to care about them and help them! Go find a child who needs help with his reading or writing. Visit someone who is stuck at home and even lonelier than you are. Helping someone else who needs it will make you feel better!" When the old man turned around, TAM was gone.

Knowing TAM had given him good advice, the old man returned from the forest. He noticed a younger fellow walking toward the path. Seeing a sly smile on the young man's face, the old man stopped to speak. "Got a problem, young fellow?" asked the old man.

The young man said, "I'm looking for the small one they call TAM. Have you seen him?"

The old man replied, "Yes, I was just talking to him. If you've got a problem, TAM's your man!"

"That's what I heard," smiled the young man. "I have big plans for old TAM!"

"What do you mean?" asked the old man. "What kind of plans?"

The young fellow flashed his sly smile. "Just think of the money to be made if I could get him out of the forest. What people would pay for his advice!"

The old man saw the end of a rope sticking out of the back of the young man's pants. This upset him very much, but he just nodded and continued on his way. Realizing what the other man planned to do, the old man knew he needed to get help.

As he got to the edge of town, the old man yelled, "Everybody, listen! TAM is in trouble! We have to help him!"

When the old man called, nearly everyone in the town came. As they hurried to the forest to help TAM, the old man explained what he had seen. As the villagers reached the path, the young fellow came walking out with TAM.

TAM was all bound up in the fellow's rope, wrapped so tightly that he could hardly be seen. The entire town stood together and demanded that TAM be released. "Let him go! We need TAM in the forest to help us with our problems!"

"Not a chance," yelled the young fellow. "There's money to be made from the advice he gives!"

– 66 –

Then, TAM spoke up with his booming voice. "If it's money for my advice that you want, you are very much out of luck," he said. "I do not give advice. I just listen."

The young man glared at the bundle of rope holding TAM. The tiny man went on, "The voice people hear is not mine. It is truly their own. When they think about their problems and listen to their conscience, they can solve their own problems quite well."

In a fury, the young man tore at the ropes that bound TAM. But when the rope unraveled, TAM had disappeared!

The young fellow was furious that there was no fortune to be had. But as he fled the forest, the townspeople were happy. Yes, they all heard TAM's words. Some believed what TAM had said, and some did not. But they all intended to return to the forest. Whether he was real or a figment, the Answer Man always seemed to know best.

Postcards from Pismo: Timeline of Important Events

written by Summer York
illustrated by Dion Williams

The following is a timeline of eight important events that occur in Michael Scotto's novel *Postcards from Pismo*.

- **June 13: Felix hears back from the soldier, Lieutenant Marcus Greene.**

Felix is very excited that Lt. Marcus Greene wrote back to him. This event shapes the story because the entire book is made up of Felix's letters to Marcus. Felix does not have many friends, so he seems like a lonely kid. Writing to Marcus almost every day gives Felix an outlet for his feelings. In fact, Marcus is the only person in whom Felix confides. Throughout the story, Felix tells Marcus about the good and bad things that happen. He even asks Marcus for advice.

- **July 18: Quin enlists in the National Guard.**

When Felix's older brother, Quin, enlists in the National Guard, Felix reacts badly. Quin and their parents have a fight, so Felix immediately emails Marcus with the subject line "HELP URGENT." After talking with Marcus about his job in Afghanistan, Felix knows that being a soldier is a dangerous job. Felix writes to Marcus about the worry he feels for his brother. He does not think Quin will be careful as a soldier. He even asks Marcus to talk to Quin. When Marcus responds, he tells Felix that he should talk to his parents first when he gets upset.

- **August 13: Felix has a panic attack during Quin's enlistment ceremony.**

Felix wants to try to be brave like Marcus. He wants to face his fears, but he has a panic attack and cries during Quin's enlistment ceremony. At first, he does not tell Marcus about it because he is ashamed. He thinks that Marcus will not want to talk to him anymore because he cried. However, Felix admits what happened on his next postcard to Marcus and resolves to be braver. This inspires him to go to the arcade at the Promenade. Felix usually avoids the Promenade because the school bully, Roger, hangs out there. However, when Felix goes, he has a good time playing with Kenneth and Lupe. He is sorry that he had not tried to be brave earlier in the summer.

- **August 26: Roger squirts Felix with pier water.**

Felix meets Kenneth and Lupe several more times to play air hockey at the arcade. One day, Roger, Kenneth, and Lupe find Felix in the arcade. Roger squirts him with a Super Soaker filled with dirty pier water. The others laugh at him and call him "Fish Stick." Felix feels very angry and discouraged. He regrets ever going to the Promenade. Furthermore, he does not like the advice that his parents give him and wishes that Quin were there to help. Felix also does not like Marcus's advice to hold his head high, and he responds with a bad attitude. After some thought, however, he apologizes to Marcus and is thankful for his help.

- **September 6: Felix punches Roger and makes him cry.**

Felix is frustrated by Roger's bullying, and he does not want to just hold his head high, as Marcus suggested. When Roger tries to take Felix's camera, Felix turns and punches Roger in the nose. When Roger starts to cry, Felix stops being mad at him. Instead, Felix feels sorry for Roger, especially when Roger's father yells at his son and says mean things to him. Felix admits that he never thought about why Roger acts the way he does. Still, Felix is suspended from school for fighting. He has never gotten into trouble at school. He worries what his teachers will think of him.

- **September 14: Marcus gets injured in Afghanistan.**

It has been about a week since Felix has heard from Marcus. Felix thinks that Marcus has stopped talking to him because Felix admitted to crying at the enlistment ceremony. Mostly, Felix is hurt because he has come to depend on Marcus to listen and give advice. When Marcus stops writing, Felix feels abandoned and says that everything that has happened is Marcus's fault. A week after Felix decides to stop writing to Marcus, he learns that Marcus has been injured in Afghanistan. Felix feels terrible for writing mean things to Marcus and blaming him for not responding.

- **September 26: Felix follows Quin's map and sees horses on the beach.**

Felix admits that the day he punched Roger was the worst day of his life. He feels like he let his family down, and he does not have anyone to talk to about it. He decides to open Quin's special letter. Inside the envelope are a map and instructions. Felix follows the map and comes to a part of the beach near the Telosa Family Ranch. To his delight, he sees people riding horses on the beach. He writes, "I forgot about the problems on my mind" and "It's good to feel understood." He finally has a place where he can go to feel happy and escape his problems.

- **October 24: Felix has his classmates make postcards for injured soldiers at Walter Reed.**

Talking to Marcus while he recovers in the hospital has made Felix realize that there are many other injured soldiers at the Walter Reed Medical Center. They all could use some cheering up. Felix wants his classmates to send postcards to injured soldiers. Felix and his mom create the postcards, and Felix and his classmates write notes on them to the soldiers. Throughout the story, Felix has relied on Marcus for help and support with the events in his life. With this project, however, Felix finds a way to help Marcus and the other soldiers who need it.

Works Cited

Scotto, Michael. *Postcards from Pismo*. Midlandia Press, 2012.

The Old Man and the Magical Deer

written by Jill Fisher
illustrated by Dion Williams

Once upon a time there lived a little old man and his little old wife. They watched out and took care of each other. They did not have much. Their clothes were old and worn. They lived in a small shack deep in the woods. The tiny home had a little living room. At night they put blankets on the floor and the living room became the bedroom. There was a tiny kitchen and a bathroom. The only food they had came from the old man. He grew a garden and went hunting. The little old wife did not help with the food. She expected her husband to take care of everything.

One day while hunting, the old man saw the most beautiful deer in the distance. It was a buck with long antlers that were like thick, strong tree branches. He looked elegant and mighty. The old man grew very excited and thought that he and his wife would have food all winter from such an animal. However, the strangest thing happened. The buck shouted to the old man, "Please do not shoot me! I am a magical deer."

The old man was in shock and did not know what to think. He turned as white as a ghost. "Do not be afraid; I will not hurt you," the buck said. With that, the kind old man decided to let the animal run away.

That afternoon the old man went home empty-handed. His hungry wife was as angry as a hornet because he did not bring any food home. Then the old man told her the story of the magical deer. His wife responded, "Did you ask him to grant you a wish?"

"Well, no, I never thought of that," the old man replied.

"First thing tomorrow, you go back to the woods and find the magical deer," the wife instructed. "I want you to order him to give us a much larger, beautiful home filled with plenty of food and new clothes. He must give you this in return for saving his life."

The old man did not agree with his wife's demands. However, he did not want to make her upset, so he went to the woods in search of the talking buck. He went to the same spot as the day before and yelled:

"Enchanted deer deep in the woods,

Come speak to me if you could.

My wife has a favor to ask of you.

I need your help; please come into view!"

A few minutes later, the buck peeked from behind a tree. "What can I do for you?" he asked.

"I'm sorry to bother you," the old man began, "but my wife thinks I should have asked you for a favor in exchange for letting you run free yesterday."

"That sounds fair," the deer replied. "I will grant her a wish."

"Oh, thank you," sighed the old man. "She will be so pleased. She would like a new, larger, beautiful house filled with attractive clothes and delicious food."

The buck granted the wish.

The kind old man thanked the magical animal and headed home. He was thrilled to see his wife. He just knew she would be overjoyed and love their new home. When he approached the area where his shack once stood he could not believe his eyes. Now there was a gorgeous stone house with colorful flowers in the yard. It was prettier than a painting. He ran into the house and threw his arms around his wife.

The old woman was not as excited, though. She wanted four bedrooms, not three. She preferred to have a fireplace in the living room, not the dining room. She felt that her new kitchen was too small and thought she deserved a larger one. The wife told her husband, "Go back to the magical deer and demand a bigger and better home. Tell him to give us what we deserve!"

The old man felt terrible. He could not believe how greedy his wife was being. But he did not want to disappoint her and wanted to make her happy, so he agreed to find the buck once more. The next morning at dawn he returned to the woods and yelled:

"Enchanted deer deep in the woods,

Come speak to me if you could.

My wife has a favor to ask of you.

I need your help; please come into view."

A few minutes later the buck came dashing toward the old man. "What's wrong?" the buck asked. "Don't you like your new home?"

The old man felt ashamed to ask for more. However, he knew his wife would be furious if he did not. "Magical deer," the man said timidly, "I love our new house. However, my wife does not. She said it is not nice enough for her. She says that you must give us what we deserve."

The wise buck thought for a few minutes before he spoke. He finally said, "You are right, old man. I did not give the two of you what you deserve. I will do so now."

With that, he granted the selfish wife's last wish.

The old man headed home. To his surprise, he found that their new, beautiful home was gone. It was not replaced by another home. All that was left where the house once stood was an old, ugly crow on the ground.

The man approached the crow, but it squawked angrily and flew off. He did not understand. Why had he lost his home? And where was his wife?

The old man walked to a stream to get a drink and clear his head. He was amazed when he looked into the water. He did not see his old, wrinkled face reflecting in it. He saw a new image with black shining eyes and a brown, spotted coat. He stared at the water, and then realized, "I have been turned into a deer!"

He did not know what to think. After a moment, the magical deer walked up behind the new buck. "What have you done to me?" asked the old man.

The magical deer explained, "You deserve to be happy, so I have turned you into one of my kind. Now you can live wild and free in the wide open forest. As for your wife, I turned her into a crow. Now she can sit and squawk all day long. She can demand things from the other crows."

Together the two strong bucks raced like lightning through the forest. The old man never looked back and he lived happily ever after.

Dinner is Served

written by Katie Catanzarite

When you grow up in an Italian family, mealtime is one of the most important times of the day. In Lucy's family, it was no different. On Sundays, her family always gathered at her grandparents' house for dinner. In the winter, her grandmother made spaghetti with plump, juicy meatballs. In the summer, her grandfather picked fresh zucchini from his own garden. He sliced them into strips, patted them with flour, dipped them in egg yolk, and tossed them in breadcrumbs and Parmesan cheese. **After** that, he fried them in lots of olive oil.

However, Lucy's favorite dinner was homemade pizza. She was eight years old when she was **finally** allowed to help her mother and grandmother in the kitchen. **Beforehand**, Lucy's mother pulled Lucy onto her lap. She wove Lucy's long hair into a braid. "Hair is not an ingredient in pizza," her grandmother would say. **Then**, Lucy had to put on an apron. Her mother helped her tie the strings into a bow behind her back. **Last**, Lucy had to wash her hands. She made sure to wash under her fingernails.

Finally, Lucy was ready to help. She climbed upon a chair next to her grandmother at the kitchen table. Today, they were going to make two large pizzas. Both grandmother and granddaughter dusted their hands in flour and prepared to roll the pizza dough. The dough was oily and sticky. Lucy kept getting holes in the dough when she tried to roll it out. Her grandmother showed her a trick. If they dusted the rolling pin with flour, the dough would not stick or tear as much.

Soon, they had rolled the dough into a nice, round circle. **Now** they were ready for the toppings. Lucy quickly discovered that this was her favorite part. She and her grandmother made a pizza with red sauce. Her mother worked on the pizza with white cream sauce. Lucy had to let her grandmother spread the sauce. They both knew it would be a mess if Lucy did it

herself. **After** her grandmother had evenly spread the red sauce, she let Lucy handle the rest of the toppings.

First, Lucy chose to add mozzarella cheese. Lucy liked a lot of cheese on her pizza.

She put so much on that it almost completely hid the sauce. **Then**, she chose the bag of pepperoni. She arranged the pepperoni into an L shape on top of the shreds of cheese so that everyone would know that she helped make the pizza. **Last**, she sprinkled some mushrooms and black olives. Her grandmother thought it looked delicious already.

Then, it was time for the pizzas to go in the oven. Lucy had to stand back as her mother slid the pizzas inside. They had to cook for 20 minutes. Lucy turned the dial on the timer and waited eagerly. **In the meantime**, she helped her grandmother clean up the kitchen. When the timer **finally** dinged, Lucy was excited. Her mother took the pizzas out of the oven. She set them on a cooling rack. The crusts were golden brown, and Lucy's L-shaped pepperoni was sizzling and crispy.

At last, Lucy ran from the kitchen and got the rest of her family. Dinner was served.

It's a Dog's Life

written by Debbie Parrish
illustrated by Doyle Daigle

Just after Little Dog's birthday, he and his family moved to a new part of town. Little Dog had gotten a new laptop computer for his birthday. He was so thrilled that you could hear his howls of joy for miles. He immediately went to his room to set up his page on LapBook, a social networking site.

First off, he made his brother one of his LapBook friends, and then he added both of his parents. It was such fun for Little Dog that he began adding all of the dogs from his old neighborhood. The more "friends" he added to his LapBook site, the more excited he got!

Mother and Father Dog said to Little Dog, "Why don't you go outside and play? You need to meet some new dogs."

Little Dog replied, "I will later. Right now I am talking to my friends online."

One day, a big dog from down the street stopped by. "I thought you might like to go for a walk," Big Dog told Little Dog.

But Little Dog said, "I will another day, thank you. Today I am busy on my computer."

"You really need to get out and run around the neighborhood, Little Dog," said his older brother. "You are getting very out of shape staying on that computer all the time. Everyone needs to get exercise to stay healthy. Besides, how are you ever going to meet any new friends here?"

"I will," promised Little Dog. "I just need to get a few more LapBook friends signed up first."

Another morning, the dog next door came by Little Dog's house and said, "Would you like to go with me to see my friend Hound Dog? He broke his paw and is having to stay off of it for a while. I'm going to go over and try to cheer him up. I thought we might play some board games with him."

Little Dog said, "No thanks, I'm going to just hang around here and find out what's happening on LapBook. I have so many friends who I need to find out about."

Day after day, Little Dog was reminded and invited to get out of the house, get some exercise, and meet new friends. But every day he just continued to find more excuses to stay on his computer. He now had over one hundred LapBook friends.

Then, one day, Little Dog felt a tingling in his legs. "Oh no," he yelped. "My legs have gone to sleep!" He decided that maybe it was a good idea to get out of the house and walk some.

He went to the park and saw a group of dogs he had added as friends on his LapBook page. "Hi," said Little Dog to one of them. "What's up?"

The other dog said, "We were just leaving to go to a birthday party for one of our friends. Bye!" And the small group of dogs trotted away.

Little Dog thought to himself, "That would have been fun. I wonder why I wasn't invited."

Then Little Dog spotted a couple of dogs across the park. Again, he recognized them from pictures on his LapBook list. He trotted over and found them playing chase.

"May I play, too?" asked Little Dog.

"We don't know you!" they said. "We're not allowed to play with strangers."

Little Dog looked puzzled. "But you are my friend on LapBook," he whined.

"That's different," one dog said.

"We don't really know you," said another.

Quickly the dogs ran away, leaving Little Dog all alone. Little Dog decided to just go home. He walked down the street toward his house. When he passed the big yellow house on the corner, there was a young dog outside with his paw wrapped in a bandage. He was limping as he walked.

"What happened to you?" Little Dog asked.

The dog replied, "I broke my paw. The vet is finally letting me outside to walk on it. I was so bored stuck inside."

Then Little Dog realized that this dog must be Hound Dog. He remembered the day he was asked to go and visit him. Little Dog felt ashamed that he had not come. He started to think about how many dogs he really knew in his new neighborhood and could not come up with even one name.

Hound Dog said, "I'd better go inside now. Mom told me not to stay out very long. Would you like to come in and have some treats with me?"

Little Dog did not hesitate. "Yes, I sure would! Then, maybe, we could play some board games!"

Little Dog had learned a valuable lesson: To have a friend, you have to be one!

Birthday Parties and Basketballs

written by Katie Catanzarite

No kids were invited to Cadence Scott's birthday party.

Yet, here 10-year-old Thomas found himself. He was sweating and itching in dress clothes and a clip-on tie. He held a present wrapped in shiny purple paper. His mom had made him go to the pink aisle in the toy store to get it. She and Cadence Scott's mother were both on the PTA.

The Scotts lived in a giant white house just one street over from Thomas. He'd never been inside. He almost had to stand on his toes to reach the doorbell.

The door swung open and revealed a very strange-looking Cadence Scott. Her blonde hair was piled on top of her head, and she wore a sparkly blue dress. Her eyes were sparkly, too. Her lips glistened bright red.

"Happy birthday, Cadence," Thomas said, shuffling his feet. He wished so badly to be on the basketball court with Greg and Sam instead of standing awkwardly in front of Cadence Scott.

When Cadence invited him in, Thomas realized that her house was like something out of a movie. A big glass chandelier hung from the ceiling in the entryway. A man in a black tuxedo played piano in the living room. Adults in fancy outfits were everywhere. They drank from tiny glasses and ate food off toothpicks.

There were no other kids around.

Thomas held out his present to Cadence without saying a word.

"Thanks," she said. "Come on, I'll put it in my room."

Cadence gathered up her dress with her free hand and skipped up the grand spiral staircase. Thomas followed her. They turned left at the top and ran across a catwalk that overlooked the house of guests. No one even seemed to notice Cadence and Thomas leaving.

Thomas didn't know what he'd expected Cadence's bedroom to look like, but it wasn't this. She had basketball posters of the Longhorns, the Rockets, and the Spurs. They were all taped on the walls and ceiling.

Her floor was littered with clothes and shoes. A few flat basketballs sat stacked in a corner.

"You play?" he asked.

She shrugged and started to pull bobby pins out of her hair. She tossed them right onto the floor with everything else.

"You're on the basketball team at school, right?" She scraped her hair into a ponytail and began to wipe off her makeup with a tissue.

Thomas nodded, speechless. Cadence kicked off her white, glittery shoes.

"Wait outside," Cadence said. Before Thomas could respond, he was already standing in the hallway, facing Cadence's closed door.

"I want to be on the girls' team," Cadence shouted through the door. "But Mom would never approve!" A minute later, she reopened the door. Cadence now wore blue basketball shorts and a Mavericks jersey.

"Come on, let's get out of here," she said. "You can teach me some stuff."

"But, what about—"

"They won't miss me," Cadence said.

"I thought you said your mom—"

"Maybe if I get good enough, she'll change her mind," Cadence replied. "Are you coming or not? You can stay if you want. Eat caviar, listen to my great-uncle Wilson play the piano…."

She skipped out the door. Thomas yanked off his clip-on tie and stuffed it in his pocket. He rolled up his shirtsleeves and grabbed the firmest basketball he could find before following her.

It seemed that he would get to play some basketball today after all.

My Annoying Best Friend

written by Vincent J. Scotto

"Stop it, Brody!" I yelled. My brother was annoying. He was always trying to get into my business. I was eight years old, and I couldn't be seen playing with little kids like him. When I went out on my bike, I wanted to be with kids my own age. I hated my little brother and never wanted to be around him. That October, though, everything changed.

"Slow down, Maya!" he called to me. I raced away as fast as my bike would carry me.

"Stop following me!" I said without turning around. I pedaled harder. I rolled faster and faster, like a racer speeding toward the finish line.

"I can't keep up with you!" Brody cried. I didn't care. I wanted him to leave me alone.

"So, stop trying and go home!" I screamed. I had to find a way to lose him.

Since my bike had bigger wheels, I knew it would handle bumps better. Brody knew that, too. I headed to the bumpiest place in the neighborhood: Acorn Hill. Acorn Hill gets its name from the oak trees that lean over the road and drop acorns all over it. I didn't think Brody would try to go down it, because it was too dangerous for his small wheels.

I looked back as I approached the hill. Brody was far behind, but I'm sure he saw me.

"Go home!" I yelled one last time. I leaned forward and began to glide down the hill. Gliding quickly turned into rumbling and popping as I crushed the acorns beneath my tires. I slid back and forth a little, but it wasn't anything my bike couldn't handle. I reached top speed as I hit the bottom. The base of the hill had small heaps of acorns that had rolled down and collected at the bottom, but I slid across them with ease. I kept pedaling so I could keep up my speed, but I was sure

it didn't matter anymore. I thought that all the way up until I heard the screaming.

It was nothing like I'd ever heard before. First, a loud clang rang out. Then, silence. Then, wailing. I turned to look back, and Brody was on the ground at the bottom of the hill. I couldn't even see his bike. I hit the brakes hard and screeched to a stop.

"Brody!" I yelled. "Are you all right?"

But he didn't hear me over his cries. I pedaled back as quickly as my legs would take me. The screams grew louder as I approached the wreck.

"Maya!" he sobbed. "Maya! Maya!" He had cuts on his arms and legs, but he was wearing his helmet, so his head seemed to be all right. There were acorns stuck to his whole body.

"Are you OK?"

"Maya, it hurts! It hurts!"

I began to pluck the acorns off his body.

"You know you can't go down Acorn Hill yet, right?"

"I know," he sniveled as he began to calm down, "but I…I had to try."

"Why did you try to follow me?"

"I was just…trying to…show you…I'm big enough to…play with you."

I felt a pain in my stomach. It was my fault. If I'd just let him play with me, he wouldn't have hurt himself.

"We have to get you home. Can you walk?"

"I don't know…." He started to cry again. I helped him to his feet. "Ow!"

"It's fine, Brody. I'll help you get home."

As we walked back to our house, I wondered how I was going to explain it to our mom. It was my fault, and I was going to be in trouble. Mom was always saying I needed to let Brody play with me. If she found out that I was trying to avoid him and he got hurt, I was going to be in big trouble. I'd be grounded, or maybe worse!

"What are you going to tell Mom?" I asked him.

"I'm gonna tell her the truth."

I was certain I'd be in big trouble. She always believed Brody, even when he exaggerated. I hoped he wouldn't tell tall tales like he usually did. We walked into our house and found Mom in the kitchen washing dishes.

"You kids already back from playing?" she asked without turning around.

"Yea. Brody got hurt so we came home."

She turned quickly and gasped at the sight.

"Brody!" she squealed, running to hug him. "Are you all right?"

"I'm fine, Mom. Just a few cuts and bruises."

Mom turned to me and grimaced. "Where were you? Weren't you watching him?"

"It happened so fast…" I began.

"Or were you ignoring him again?" she interrupted. I froze.

"It was my fault, Mom," Brody said. "I wanted to show Maya that I'm brave, so I went down Acorn Hill. I fell off my bike and she hurried to help me. If she hadn't been there, I'd still be stuck out on the hill. Maya saved me!"

My mother became at ease. "I'm so glad you're finally taking some responsibility for your brother, Maya. Let's get you cleaned up, Brody."

With that, they headed to the bathroom. Brody turned and winked at me. I smiled back at him and gave a thumb up. From then on, if I wasn't with my friends, I let Brody tag along with me. He was still annoying sometimes, but that was all right. We became great friends over time. In fact, he just might be my best friend.

The Legend of the No Face Doll

adapted by Debbie Parrish
illustrated by Doyle Daigle

Many years ago, there were three sisters. These sisters were spirits known as the sustainers of life. Their job was to feed and support life. The sister spirits were named Corn, Beans, and Squash. The Spirit of the Corn felt lucky to be a sustainer of life. She wished to help her people live well and be happy.

One day, the Spirit of the Corn observed that her people, the Iroquois tribe, had to work very hard just to survive. They hunted, fished, gathered food, and labored to build and protect their homes. "I want to do something to make my people's work easier," the Corn Spirit said, "but I do not know what to do."

The Spirit of the Corn asked the Creator to help her. The Creator told her to take some of her own cornhusk and make a doll. When the spirit finished, the Creator made for the doll a beautiful face and gave it life.

Gratefully, the Corn Spirit left with the living doll. When they reached their home, the Corn Spirit told the Cornhusk Doll that she would have a very special job to do. She was to go from village to village and play with the children. The doll would play games, sing songs, and tell stories to the children to make them happy.

"The adults will take cheer in the joyous laughter of the boys and girls," explained the Spirit of the Corn. "It will remind them why they are working so hard. They are trying to make a good life for their children. The adults will be happy and the work will seem much easier."

The Cornhusk Doll set out to do her job. Everything went well in the first village. She told stories as the young ones listened in delight. The children loved her games and songs so much that the air was full of laughter. When the grownups heard this, they were very pleased. Their work did become easier, and they labored with smiles on their faces. As the Cornhusk Doll moved on to the next village, every adult thanked her for making the children happy. They also told her that she was very beautiful.

In the next village, the experience of the Cornhusk Doll was much the same. The children laughed loudly as she sang, told stories, and played with them. The adults felt happy and content to be working hard for the sake of the children.

"Thank you so much for reminding us why we work so hard," said almost every villager. "We think you are quite beautiful."

Over and over, in village after village, the Cornhusk Doll heard praise for her beauty. One day, while on her way to the next village, she stopped by a lake to rest. She looked into the water, and there she saw her reflection. The Cornhusk Doll was quite pleased with the lovely face she saw looking back at her.

"Oh! I do have a pretty face!" the Cornhusk Doll said. "This is what the people have been telling me!" She smiled and continued to admire herself in the water until she lost all track of time.

The village children who had come to look forward to her visits thought that the Cornhusk Doll had forgotten them. They began to cry. The Spirit of the Corn heard the cries of the children and went to find the doll.

"You have forgotten your job," the Corn Spirit told her. "You are supposed to be making the children laugh. Instead, they are crying."

Many times the Cornhusk Doll promised the Spirit of the Corn that she would not forget again. Again and again, though, she stopped by the lake to admire her own beauty. Time would pass as she gazed into the water. All the while, she would smile and say, "I have the most beautiful face in the world."

The Spirit of the Corn was disappointed. She went to visit the Cornhusk Doll once more.

"You have not behaved well and have not taken care of your responsibilities," the Spirit of the Corn scolded.

"Every action has a consequence. If you choose to act with such vanity again, you will learn what I mean."

Of course, the Cornhusk Doll pledged again to be more responsible. She vowed not to think so much about her beauty. But the Cornhusk Doll just could not keep her promise. After some time, she stopped by the lake once more. When she peered into the water to admire herself, she discovered the consequence of her behavior. In the water, she saw no reflection. She could no longer see her own lovely face.

Even today, when an Iroquois mother makes her child a doll, it has no face. She tells her children the story of the Cornhusk Doll and reminds them to be responsible. They must never think they are better than anyone else, because everyone has special gifts.

The Perfect Pair

written by Vincent J. Scotto

Harold hadn't always been a confident boy. He was regularly picked last to play games at the park; often, he didn't even try to join in. He usually went to the swings. At least he didn't have to compete with anyone there. Harold didn't mind playing alone, but things were about to change in a way that he never could have expected.

One hot evening in July, Harold went to the park as usual. Some of the neighborhood kids were already playing kickball, so he went directly for the swing set. Something was different, though; someone was already there, swinging away. When Harold approached, he was able to see more clearly that it was someone he hadn't met. Stranger still, it was the kind of person who frightened him the most: a girl.

When Harold came close, he quickly jumped on the second swing without looking directly at the girl. He hoped that she wouldn't say anything. She laughed a little.

"I'm Genesis," she said confidently. Harold remained quiet. "What's your name?"

"Are you talking to me?" Harold asked as he began to swing higher. He was trying to avoid her.

"Who else would I be talking to if you're the only one around? You can call me Gen for short."

"I'm Harold," he said timidly, "but you can call me Harry. Did you just move here?"

"Yeah," she replied. "I was going to play with the other kids, but I don't really know anyone yet."

"That's all right," Harold said. "I don't play with them much either. I prefer swinging."

Genesis giggled. "I guess we can be loners together!" she proclaimed. "What do you think?"

"Sounds good to me," Harold said as he smiled. "But how can two people be loners?"

"All right, we'll be the Perfect Pair!" she exclaimed, pointing to the sky.

"Even better!" Harold agreed.

The two kids met at the park every day to swing on the swing set. They spent each afternoon laughing and soaring. They talked about their families, shared secrets, and challenged each other to swinging contests. They soon became great friends. Harold couldn't have been happier, but something was about to mess up everything.

One day, when Harold had plans to meet Genesis, he was running a bit late. He had to clean his room before his grandmother would allow him to go to the park. By the time Harold arrived, he found that Genesis was already there on the swings. This time, however, she was with another boy. The new boy, Bryan, had moved to town in September. Harold didn't really know him, but Bryan was much bigger, and that scared Harold a bit. Harold had never dared to approach him, but now he'd have to if he wanted to swing with Genesis.

"Hey, Gen," Harold said softly.

"Harry!" she said. "Where have you been? I was waiting for a bit, but then Bryan came over."

Bryan stopped swinging and said, "What's up, dude?"

Harold grimaced at Bryan and turned to Genesis. "I thought we were swinging today."

"You snooze you lose, dude!" Bryan laughed.

"We can all hang out," Genesis insisted. "Right, Bryan?"

"There are only two swings!" Bryan said. "You're just going to have to find something else to do."

"Gen and I always swing," Harold said in a shaky voice. Bryan got off the swing and came very close to Harold. Bryan stood tall and looked down at him.

"I said beat it, dude." Bryan shoved Harold backward.

Harold hit the ground hard, tears welling up in his eyes.

"Ha!" Bryan teased. "Are you gonna cry now?"

Genesis jumped to her feet. "Leave him alone!"

Harold stood up, brushing the wood chips off his legs and shirt.

"You can't push him around like that," she scolded.

"I was just trying to get him to leave…."

"I don't want him to leave!" Genesis interrupted.

Harold smiled and raised his eyebrow at Bryan.

"Harry is my friend, and if you don't like it, maybe you should leave." Genesis pointed toward the field, where the other kids were playing football.

"I get it," Bryan said. "You win this one, dude." Bryan jogged over toward the football game. "You guys got room for one more?" he called out.

Harold smiled at Genesis. "Thanks," he said, relieved.

"No problem," she reassured him. "Just show up when you're supposed to next time!"

"Well, I had to clean my room."

"I bet you had dirty socks everywhere! Ew!"

They both laughed.

"We're always going to be friends, right, Gen?"

"Of course we are. As long as we have a set of swings, we'll always be the Perfect Pair!"

The two jumped on the swings and played the rest of the afternoon. They stayed friends for the rest of their lives, just like Genesis promised. The Perfect Pair was even more perfect than they could have ever thought possible, and nothing came between them again.

Anansi and the River: An Ashanti Folktale

adapted by Vincent J. Scotto

One day, Anansi the Spider went for a walk. He went deep into the African forest. He did not tell anyone in the Ashanti village where he was going. He didn't even tell his six sons. At night, he became lost. He came upon a river and saw a glowing light. Leaning closer to see, he fell into the water. Anansi grabbed the ball of light in his hands. Before Anansi could climb out of the river, though, he was swallowed by a fish.

Each of Anansi's sons had special abilities. Anansi's first son could see trouble with his mind. He saw that Anansi had fallen into the river.

"My brothers!" he said. "Father is in trouble. We must find him."

Anansi's second son could build roads. He built a road to the river. The brothers travelled the road to save Anansi.

"He's in the water!" his first son cried. Anansi's third son could dry up rivers. He sucked up all the water in the river.

"Help me!" Anansi yelled from inside the fish. Luckily, his fourth son had the ability to skin animals. His fourth son cut open the fish, and Anansi came tumbling out.

"Thank you, my sons!" Anansi said. But just as he was getting to his feet, a hawk swooped down and grabbed him. The hawk carried him away. "Help me, my sons!"

Anansi's fifth son was a powerful stone-thrower. He picked up a stone and threw it at the hawk. The stone hit the hawk in the eye! Anansi fell through the air, toward the ground.

"Catch me, my sons!" Anansi yelped. "Catch me!"

"Thank you, my sons!" Anansi said happily.

Anansi and his sons went back to their village. They had a great party. Anansi wanted to repay them, but he only had the one ball of light. His sons argued over who should have the prize. Soon, the Ashanti villagers took sides.

"I should have it," his first son said. "I'm the one who knew you were in trouble."

"I should have it," his second son said. "I built the road to find you."

"I should have it," his third son said. "I dried up the river to get you."

"I should have it," his fourth son said. "I cut open the fish to save you."

"I should have it," his fifth son said. "I stopped the hawk from carrying you away."

"I should have it," his sixth son said. "I caught you when you fell."

Anansi could not decide. He went back into the forest to ask the Ashanti Spirit for help.

"I will hold the light for all to see," the Spirit said. "Each night, everyone will see the light. All of your sons will be honored."

Anansi accepted the offer. He gave the Ashanti Spirit the ball of light, and the Spirit placed it in the night sky. That is how the world got the moon.

Works Cited

Elder, John and Hertha D. Wong, editors. *Family of Earth and Sky: Indigenous Tales of Nature from Around the World.* Beacon Press, 1994.

McDermott, Gerald. *Anansi the Spider: A Tale from the Ashanti.* Henry Holt & Company, 1973.

Aunt Nancy and the Swamp: A Southern American Folktale

adapted by Vincent J. Scotto

One hot evening in South Carolina, Aunt Nancy took a walk into the woods. She walked farther than she ever had before. Eventually, it became dark, and she could not find her way home. Aunt Nancy saw a light coming from the Four Holes Swamp. She approached the edge to get a closer look. The light came from a glowing ball. She reached to grab the ball of light, but she fell in her attempt. She grabbed the light, but she was quickly gobbled up by an alligator.

Aunt Nancy's six nephews became worried. Her oldest nephew could sense that the trouble was coming from the woods.

"We're sure to find Aunt Nancy at the swamp!" he declared.

"I will take us there!" the second-oldest nephew said. He had several fast horses.

Aunt Nancy's nephews rode into the woods, toward the swamp. When they reached the swamp, her third-oldest nephew had an idea. "I will dry up the swamp!" he declared.

When the swamp dried up, they found the alligator at the bottom.

"I will take care of this!" the third-youngest nephew said. He was an expert skinner. He cut open the alligator and pulled out Aunt Nancy.

"Thank you, my nephews!" she said excitedly. As she cleaned herself off, she was suddenly taken away by a golden eagle. "Help me!" she cried. The golden eagle soared high into the night sky.

"I'll save you, Aunt Nancy!" the second-youngest nephew yelled. He was an expert rock-thrower. He hit the golden eagle in the beak with a rock. The eagle let go of Aunt Nancy. She fell out of the sky and screamed, "Help me!"

"I'll save you!" the youngest nephew said. He ran underneath her and caught her with his great arms.

"Thank you, my nephews!" Aunt Nancy proclaimed. "Thank you all!"

The family returned to Aunt Nancy's home. She decided that they deserved the light for saving her. However, they could not agree who should have it.

"I should have the light," the oldest nephew said. "I knew where to find you in the swamp."

"I should have the light," the second-oldest nephew said. "My horses carried us to save you."

"I should have the light," the third-oldest nephew said. "I dried up the swamp to find you."

"I should have the light," the third-youngest nephew said. "I saved you from the alligator's belly."

"I should have the light," the second-youngest nephew said. "I saved you from the golden eagle's clutches."

"It should be mine," the youngest nephew said. "I caught you when you fell from the sky."

Aunt Nancy couldn't decide. She went into the woods to think. She was visited by a great spirit. Aunt Nancy asked the spirit for guidance.

"If your nephews cannot share the light," the spirit said, "I will hold it where all can see."

"That will solve the problem," Aunt Nancy agreed.

The spirit placed the light in the sky. Aunt Nancy's nephews saw it glowing at night, high above. They agreed that it was a fair way to share the light. From then on, everyone saw the light in the night sky. That is how the moon came to light up the night.

Works Cited

"Aunt-nancy." *Project Gutenberg Self-Publishing Press*. World Library Foundation, self.gutenberg.org/articles/aunt_nancy. Accessed 11 Feb. 2018.

Elder, John and Hertha D. Wong, editors. *Family of Earth and Sky: Indigenous Tales of Nature from Around the World*. Beacon Press, 1994.

Jasmine and the Song

written by Jill Fisher
illustrated by Dion Williams

Not that long ago in a place called Dollyland, there lived a girl named Jasmine. She was an ordinary young girl, but she had grown bored with her common life. She desired more. She longed to be famous. Jasmine wanted everyone to know her name.

Oftentimes Jasmine would daydream of fame and fortune. She dreamed of walking the red carpet in fancy dresses. She imagined owning a big house with lots of bedrooms and bathrooms. Jasmine thought a pool with a water slide would be perfect in the backyard. When she became famous, she would hire a few people to make her life easier—like someone to cook her food. She would also like someone to pick out her fancy clothes.

The more and more Jasmine dreamed about these things, the more she wanted to become famous. Only she didn't know how. What was her talent? She was not very good at dancing. Could she learn to play an instrument? She had always liked the piano. After thinking for a long time, she came up with a plan. Jasmine knew just who to ask for help. She went to visit Diva, the goddess of fame, to see what she could do.

The goddess Diva told Jasmine that she had to do something amazing to become famous. Diva said to practice singing so that she could perform a beautiful song. She told the young girl that it would take a lot of hard work, but not to give up. The goddess promised that if Jasmine wrote a song, Diva would do the rest. The moment anyone heard Jasmine's song, they would fall in love with it. Jasmine was grateful for the help. She would learn to sing a beautiful song and Diva would make her rich and famous.

A few months went by. Jasmine practiced singing the whole time. However, it was much harder than she thought it would be. She felt like she would never sing a beautiful song on her own. Then, Jasmine remembered a beautiful sound she had heard earlier. It was in the park. She had heard a shy girl with a stunning voice, singing the most beautiful song. It gave Jasmine an idea.

Jasmine went to the park and secretly recorded the shy girl's song. Then she played the music and said she was the one singing! Just as Diva had promised, as soon as everyone heard this song it climbed to the top of the charts. Jasmine was famous by the end of the week!

The goddess of fame was very surprised when she heard Jasmine's song playing on the radio. She did not know that Jasmine was able to sing so well. Diva couldn't wait to congratulate her.

The goddess Diva went to visit Jasmine. On the way to Jasmine's fancy new house, Diva walked through the park. There, she heard the most beautiful singing. At first, she thought it was Jasmine singing, because it sounded exactly like her song from the radio. However, it was someone else. It was a girl she had never met, staring at the ground and singing her heart out. Diva listened to the girl's voice and realized what Jasmine had done. She had stolen this girl's song and claimed it as her own.

When the goddess of fame arrived at Jasmine's house, she told her how much she loved her song on the radio. Diva asked Jasmine to sing it for her. The young girl said her throat hurt and it was not a good time to sing. Then Diva told Jasmine that she knew about the shy girl in the park. Jasmine started to cry. She admitted to cheating to become famous. Diva became furious. Before she went away, the goddess promised Jasmine that she would regret her lies.

Jasmine was embarrassed that she had been caught. However, she was still happy to be famous. At least Diva had not taken that away. But it did not take long for things to change for the worse.

Being famous was not what Jasmine expected. In fact, Diva made sure it was terrible. The goddess wanted to punish Jasmine for her dishonesty. Diva made up things that were not true about Jasmine. The goddess told people that Jasmine liked to eat fish sandwiches for breakfast. Jasmine was horrified. She thought that was disgusting! She worried that people would think she was some sort of freak.

Thanks to Diva, everywhere Jasmine went people knew her name. One time when Jasmine was at the grocery store with her mom, a young girl came up behind her and cut a lock of her hair off! The girl wanted it to sell on the Internet! Jasmine was miserable. She wanted her old, plain, ordinary life back.

She talked to Diva, the goddess of fame, and begged her for forgiveness. She told her she was very sorry for tricking her and not taking her advice. Jasmine said that she would do anything for her help. Diva told the young girl that she should not lie and cheat people.

Jasmine spent the rest of her life in the spotlight. Every year she became more famous than the last. She walked the red carpet more times than she cared to remember. She spent her days lonely in her big, fancy house. It had a lot of bedrooms and bathrooms, but Jasmine did not have any friends or family to fill the large house. The only thing she dreamed of was her ordinary, common life.

– 91 –

Choosing Bedtimes: An Opinion Article

written by Mark Weimer

Parents should allow their children to choose their own bedtimes. Kids are so busy with activities that there are simply not enough hours in a day to accomplish everything. Letting children choose their own bedtimes will help them complete tasks, give them free time, and create more family time.

Today, children have a lot more to complete in a single day. Teachers pile on hours of homework each night. Kids may need to stay up later to get their work done. If they are forced to go to bed, they might not complete their schoolwork. They should be allowed to stay up later if needed. It will teach them how to set priorities.

Children are busier than ever with schoolwork, but they also need time to just be kids. They need free time to run around and play. Sadly, many schools have phased out recess. Heavy workloads and too many scheduled activities are robbing kids of their childhoods. Children need idle time. If they are permitted to stay up later, they will get that idle time.

With so much for children to juggle, what time do they have left for their families? Adults stay up late so that they can enjoy time together. Why can't children also stay up to share that time? How much time do families really spend enjoying each other's company during the school year? Children might have only a few free hours a week if they cannot choose their own bedtimes.

Being a kid is more complicated than ever. There is hardly enough time to get work done, be a kid, and enjoy time with family. Allowing children to choose their own bedtimes helps them extend their day. They can be more successful in school, have more fun, and enjoy more family time.

The Girl with the Golden Teeth

written by Katie Catanzarite
illustrated by Brittanie Markham

Abby was finally getting her braces put on, and she was miserable. She would be the only kid in the fourth grade with braces. She just knew someone was bound to call her "metal mouth."

"Now, it'll take a couple of days for your teeth to straighten out," her orthodontist, Dr. Madden, told her. "But it shouldn't be too long before the braces do their job."

"Why do I have to have them on for so long then?"

"Because braces like to be straight—that's what they're for. Teeth, on the other hand, sometimes have other plans."

"I don't mind having a crossbite," Abby said. "It helps me whistle better."

Dr. Madden laughed, and his eyes crinkled above his blue surgical mask.

"Well, you may not mind, but your gums do. I know it's scary, Abby, but you'll be just fine. You won't have to have them on for more than nine months."

"Will it hurt?" Abby asked. She remembered that nasty, gooey mold they put in her mouth to measure her teeth for braces.

"Not at all. The glue might taste funny at first, but nothing will hurt. I promise." Dr. Madden lowered her back in the chair and turned on the bright yellow light above her face. Abby opened her mouth, closed her eyes, and counted to 100.

As Dr. Madden worked on her teeth, she got more and more relaxed. He was right; it didn't hurt at all. The water they used to rinse out her mouth did taste sour,

and so did the glue, but soon Abby was too distracted by her color choices to notice. Dr. Madden held out a palette with a whole bunch of different colors, but in the end, Abby chose a metallic gold. Dr. Madden said this would be the last thing they did today. The brackets had to sit for a while, so she'd have to come back on Friday to get the wire put in.

Abby didn't care. During the whole drive home, she couldn't stop looking at her mouth in the rearview mirror.

The next day at school, Abby wasn't even worried about showing everyone her braces. All her friends were amazed, and the whole class, even the teacher, wanted to see the girl with the golden teeth.

Hydraulic Fracturing

written by Mark Weimer

Fracking is one way that gas companies collect natural gas. The word *frack* is short for "hydraulic fracturing." Hydraulic fracturing involves breaking apart rocks in the ground to release gas. First, fracking company workers drill into the ground. Then, they force a mixture of water, sand, and chemicals into the ground. This mixture breaks apart rock. The mixture contains many poisonous chemicals. Fracking has not been around long enough to know whether it can hurt water supplies. Even so, some fracking workers cut corners and are not as careful as they need to be. For these reasons, fracking should be stopped.

Fracking was once considered a safe way to collect gas. The current boom in fracking began in the early 2000s. Early studies showed that fracking did not poison water supplies. In 2005, the Safe Drinking Water Act was changed to state that fracking companies could ignore the act. Many people were puzzled by this. Nobody truly knows the long-term effects of injecting poison into the ground. If fracking was supposed to be safe, why would laws about safe drinking water not apply?

Fracking has been proven to break apart Earth's crust. In Youngstown, Ohio, drillers began to drill by a minor fault line deep underground. This drilling directly resulted in 77 earthquakes from March 4th to March 12th, 2014. The largest of these earthquakes measured a 3.0 on the Richter scale. This was neither the first nor the last time that Ohio experienced drilling-related earthquakes.

Some fracking companies have been careless about safety. In October 2014, billions of gallons of poisonous

fracking liquid were dumped into California aquifers. In 2010, 57,000 gallons of fracking liquid spilled into Pennsylvania soil. In May 2015, fracking fluids were found in the drinking water of three homes in Pennsylvania. The fracking company bought all three properties, which quickly caused an end to the complaints.

The freshwater system of the Ohio River Valley provides fresh water to the northeastern and midwestern United States. If this system were to become polluted with toxic chemicals, it would create a massive water crisis. Fracking is destroying both water supplies and Earth's crust. There are many other, safer sources of energy to use. There is no need to continue to allow fracking.

Works Cited

Atkin, Emily. "Judge Rules Exxon Must Face Criminal Charges Over 50,000 Gallon Fracking Waste Spill." *ThinkProgress.org*, 3 Jan. 2014, thinkprogress.org/climate/2014/01/03/3115991/exxon-criminal-charges-fracking-spill/. Accessed 15 Feb. 2017.

"Fracking: Laws and Loopholes." *Clean Water Action*, cleanwater.org/page/fracking-laws-and-loopholes/. Accessed 15 Feb. 2017.

Oskin, Becky. "Fracking Led to Ohio Earthquakes." *LiveScience.com*, 5 Jan. 2015, www.livescience.com/49326-fracking-caused-ohio-earthquakes.html. Accessed 15 Feb. 2017.

St. Fleur, Nicholas. "Fracking Chemicals Detected in Pennsylvania Drinking Water." *New York Times*, 5 May 2015, p. A15.

Toliver, Zachary. "Billions of gallons of fracking fluid dumped into California drinking water." *Eaglefordtexas.com*, 13 Oct. 2014, eaglefordtexas.com/news/id/136996/billions-gallons-fracking-fluid-dumped-california-drinking-water/. Accessed 15 Feb. 2017.

The Third Grade Gumshoe

written by Summer York

It was a stormy summer afternoon, and I was relaxing in my treehouse, waiting for the next case. I had my feet propped up on my makeshift desk. The distant thunder was almost lulling me to sleep when I heard a knock on the door. The girl walked in. I could tell that she had a **dilemma** and I was the only one who could help.

"You're the Third Grade **Gumshoe**, right?" she asked, twirling one of her red pigtails.

"That's what it says on the door," I replied. I adjusted my glasses and offered her a chair. As a highly **intellectual** third-grader, I ran a successful detective agency out of my backyard treehouse. There had never been a mystery I couldn't solve. However, I had an uneasy feeling that this girl had a real challenge for me.

"My name is Rosalie," she began, "and I need your help. Someone stole my favorite blue sweater that my grandma made for me. I just have to get it back. Can you find it for me?"

"I'd be happy to help, Rosalie," I assured her. "When did you last see your sweater?" I was soon scribbling

furiously on my notepad as she explained what had happened.

"Well, I was wearing it at the playground late Saturday afternoon. It was right around sunset. I took the sweater off and laid it on a bench. We were playing Freeze Tag, so I didn't want to get it dirty. When I came back for it, it was gone! There were prints in the mud all around the bench." She described the prints as looking like small, five-fingered hands.

"This is indeed a **conundrum**," I said thoughtfully.

"A what?" she asked, clearly confused.

"It's very puzzling," I clarified. "I'll contact you when I have a lead." I wrote her phone number on my notepad. "My partner will show you out," I said, pointing to the sleeping Jack Russell terrier in the corner. Rosalie gave me a strange look and then left me to get to work. Excited for a new case, Buddy—my partner—and I headed to the scene of the crime.

At the park, I located the bench in question. However, the recent rain had washed away the prints in the mud. Without any **evidence** to help me, I searched the area for other clues. I wasn't having much luck, but then I spotted something in the nearby bushes. I squatted down and pushed my **spectacles** higher on my nose to get a better look. Carefully, I unraveled a piece of blue yarn from the tangle of branches. A clue! This yarn had to be from Rosalie's blue sweater. I bagged the evidence and hurried back to my treehouse office.

Back at **headquarters**, I called Rosalie. I needed her to identify the yarn I had found. While I waited for her, I focused on the other key piece of evidence: the prints. Rosalie had said they were like small hands with five fingers. I was pretty certain that I could **eliminate** the possibility of a human. Unless it was a very small child who walked on its hands, it was very unlikely that a person stole the sweater. I had the feeling that I was dealing with an animal **perpetrator**. I went to my iPad and did some research on small, wild, five-toed animals that live in our area. Based on the playground's location, I narrowed down my list of five-toed criminals to a skunk, a raccoon, a squirrel, or a weasel.

It didn't take long for Rosalie to get to my office. "Yeah, that's from my sweater!" she shrieked in delight. I also showed her some photographs of animal footprints on my iPad. She had no doubt that the footprints she saw matched the pictures of raccoon tracks I had found online. This was the break in the case we needed! Rosalie and I went back to the playground to look for raccoon tracks.

"Ah-ha!" I exclaimed as I eyed some suspicious prints in the mud at the park's edge. Rosalie and I slowly followed the trail, which led under bushes, around trees, and down to a small creek. The tracks led away from the creek to a small **thicket** of low bushes.

"I'm willing to bet that the **culprit** is hiding in those bushes," I whispered. Silently, we crept up to the bushes and parted the cluster of branches. There was the raccoon with the blue sweater! But that wasn't all— there were also four baby raccoons nestled in the soft yarn. Apparently, the sweater thief was really a mother raccoon building a nest for her babies. Not wanting to scare them, we decided to leave the sweater and sneak away. Another difficult case had been solved by the Third Grade Gumshoe.

An Excerpt from "The Ride"

written by Jennifer Tkocs

I was lucky that my friends and I were strong riders. We'd spent all summer riding our bikes out on this trail. I guess that's how we lost track of time tonight. We were so used to hanging out and fishing late into the evening along the river. We'd forgotten that darkness falls earlier the longer summer goes on.

The thunderclaps were getting closer together now. I thought for sure that I could feel droplets of rain on my arms. My friends must have also, as all four of us got a sudden burst of speed. It wouldn't be long now.

The Ghost in the Window

written by Summer York

Today was the best day of the year: Halloween. Skylar and her friends were excited because it was the day of Skylar's annual Spook-tacular Halloween Party. Skylar's Halloween parties were epic—especially when everyone told scary stories. The group gathered in Skylar's basement, which was decorated like a haunted house. Devin came as a vampire, Tara was a ballerina, and Emmitt was dressed as some undead zombie creature. Of course, Skylar had the best costume. She was a witch with a pointy hat, long raggedy hair, and black fingernails. The guests were admiring the spooky decorations when the doorbell rang.

"Good evening, and welcome to the Spook-tacular House of Terror!" Skylar cackled in her best witch's voice. The werewolf that stood outside let out a loud howl at the Moon, followed by Todd's giggling under his mask. "Great costume," Skylar said, patting Todd's furry head and laughing.

"You too," he replied as they joined the others in the basement.

"Vhat are we going to do first?" Devin asked in a vampire accent that made everyone laugh.

"First, we're gonna play Ghost in the Graveyard," Skylar said. "In the dark?" Tara asked hesitantly.

"Oh, are you scared?" Todd teased. Emmitt started toward Tara in his best stiff zombie walk, and she shrieked. They all headed outside into Skylar's large backyard.

"All right, this tree is base," Skylar instructed. "Todd, you be 'it' first." Todd ran off to hide and quickly disappeared into the darkness. "Whoever finds Todd has to yell 'Ghost in the Graveyard,' and then we all have to run back to base. If Todd tags you before you touch base, you're 'it.'" They all split up to find Todd, except Tara, who stayed close to Skylar in the dark.

They crept silently through the blackness, lit only by the Moon. They looked behind rocks, around trees, and even inside the creepy old shed.

"I don't like this game," Tara whispered to Skylar.

"Shh!" Skylar hushed her, intent on finding Todd. Just then, Tara gasped and grabbed Skylar's arm. "What's the matter?" Skylar asked.

"I thought I saw something." She pointed to a distant group of trees. "Was it Todd?" Skylar asked mischievously.

"No, it was small and white, like a ghost," Tara said with wide eyes.

From the other side of the shed, they heard Devin yell, "Ghost in the Graveyard," and Skylar bolted for base. Tara ran, too, but she looked back toward the trees in fear. After a few more rounds of the game, it was too dark to see anything in the backyard.

"Now it's time to tell ghost stories!" Skylar announced. They went back into the basement, turned off the lights, and huddled in a circle on the floor.

"I have one!" Emmitt shouted. Skylar handed him the flashlight. He held it up to his face so that his zombie costume was even scarier. "There was this old insane asylum on a hill, and the patients took control of it, and they got a bunch of sharp swords—"

"Ew," Skylar interrupted, snatching the flashlight from Emmitt. "That's not a ghost story; that's just gross. Who has a really spooky story?"

"I'll go," Devin volunteered, taking the flashlight and beginning in a low voice. "Once, in an old cemetery, there was a crumbling headstone, like from the 1800s. The writing was so old and worn that you couldn't read it. Every night, this young girl named Mary would sit beside the headstone. No one knew where she came from or why she sat there. Then, one night, the caretaker at the cemetery noticed upturned dirt in front of the headstone. He went over to it and found that the grave had been freshly dug. On the headstone, he clearly read the words 'Here Lies Mary.'"

"Ooooo!" everyone squealed in fear and delight.

"Wait, did you hear that?" Tara quieted them, and they sat listening. Then, a rattling on the basement window made them jump.

"It's just the lilac bush branches hitting the glass," Skylar said calmly. "Now it's my turn!" She took the flashlight. "This is called 'The Ghost in the Window.'"

"Ahh!" Tara screamed, diving behind the couch and startling everyone. "What's wrong now?" Todd asked.

"I s-saw a g-g-ghost in the window!" Tara stammered as she covered her eyes in terror. "Tara, I didn't even start the story yet," Skylar complained.

"Yeah, Tara," Devin said, "it's just a story." He walked over to the window and peered into the inky blackness. "There's nothing—"

Suddenly, a crack of lightning lit up the sky and illuminated a ghostly face looking right at Devin. They all screamed and crowded behind the couch with Tara. Then, the lights flickered on in the basement as Skylar's parents came into the room.

"What is all the screaming about down here?" her mother demanded.

"We saw a ghost in the window!" Skylar explained in sheer terror. "We all saw it!"

"A ghost, huh?" Skylar's dad shook his head, turned on the backyard light, and went outside.

"Dad, no, don't go out there!" Skylar pleaded. They all held their breath, waiting to see if Skylar's dad would return unharmed. A few seconds later, they heard a scuffle of footsteps, and in walked Skylar's dad toting a real live ghost under his arm!

"You caught the ghost!" Emmitt cried. The small ghost squirmed and tried to escape. "This is no ghost, guys," Skylar's dad said. In the lights of the basement, the ghost became a bedsheet with two holes for eyes. It was wearing tennis shoes and laughing hysterically. Skylar's dad pulled off the bedsheet to reveal Reid, Skylar's prankster little brother.

"Reid!" Skylar hissed furiously. She lunged at him, but he dodged and ran up the stairs, laughing the whole way. Having solved the mystery, Skylar's parents left the kids to their party.

"Guess I'd better think of a new story," Skylar said with a nervous glance at the window.

They all tried to laugh off their fear, but they decided to leave the lights on.

Yogurt

written by Mark Weimer

Schools should serve yogurt with every school lunch. Yogurt comes from milk, which is packed with protein and vitamins. Healthy bacteria turn milk into yogurt. These same bacteria are good for the human immune system; they also help people to digest food properly. Yogurt can really benefit people who have digestion problems. The calcium in yogurt strengthens people's bones. The protein in yogurt is great for everyone's muscles. The fat in yogurt helps brain growth, especially in young children. Eating yogurt can reduce a person's chances for brain, bone, and muscle disease. Yogurt also reduces the chance of high blood pressure. It also suppresses appetite, which is helpful in the battle against obesity. It is cheap and can be made with skim milk, low-fat milk, whole milk, almond milk, or soy milk. School cafeteria workers can make fresh yogurt and add other great ingredients, such as blueberries, oats, and/or any other superfoods. Yogurt is the perfect food for a healthy brain and active body; it should be a part of every growing student's lunch.

Life in New York City

written by Jill Fisher
illustrated by Kevin Dinello

Have you ever visited a big city? If so, you probably noticed that cities are busy places. Close your eyes and picture a city. Think of all the ways a city can touch your senses. What did you imagine? Maybe you smelled the hotdogs cooking on every street corner. Perhaps you heard the loud horns of taxis and the wailing sirens of fire trucks. Or maybe you saw people everywhere, all of them in a hurry. In the city, there is something going on all of the time. In no American city is that more true than New York City.

New York City is an outstanding place to live. It is located in the state of New York. More people reside in New York City than in any other city in the United States. Over eight and a half million people call it home. New York City is an urban area, a community that has little open land and a lot of people. New York City has many fans and many nicknames. One of its nicknames is "the city that never sleeps." It earned that nickname because at any hour of the day, a person can find something fun to do there.

New York City is full of different cultures and places to visit. There are so many things to do. Many of the places are in easy walking distance. It would not take long to find a grocery store, bank, post office, or library. The city is filled with all sorts of entertainment. It is the home of two professional baseball teams, as well as a basketball team and a hockey team. Some of the most famous theaters in the world are in New York, on a long street called Broadway. You can find live music being played in town on any day of the week. In fact, many years ago New York City was nicknamed the Big Apple. Many believe it had to do with all the jazz musicians performing in the city.

The Big Apple has many other forms of entertainment as well. All kinds of museums can be found throughout the city. Often, there are festivals or parades on the busy streets. The city is full of beautiful sights as well, like skyscrapers, which are very tall buildings. It's true; you can always find something to do in New York City. Many visitors like to go to Ellis Island or take a ferry ride to see the Statue of Liberty. Others climb to the top of the Empire State Building. No matter what you like to do or how old you are, there is something for everyone to enjoy.

If you get hungry during all of the excitement, don't worry. When it comes to food, New York City has a restaurant for every taste. You don't have to travel the world to try different types of foods such as Italian, Mexican, Chinese, and many more. You only need to walk a few blocks. Living in New York City is amazing.

If you like the outdoors, New York City has many beautiful parks to visit. Central Park is the most famous one. Families can do many wonderful outdoor activities there. They can fish, ride bicycles, take a carriage ride, swim, or even go ice skating. On any day you will find people enjoying the green grass, trees, and fresh air.

There are many ways to travel around New York City. Most people who live in the Big Apple do not own cars. If the place you would like to go is too far

to walk, you could call a taxi. Some people prefer to ride the bus or subway. A subway is a train that travels underground. You will even see people riding bicycles through the city. No matter which way you travel, it is a good idea to carry a map so that you don't get lost in the hectic city.

There are some things not everyone enjoys about living in New York City. First of all, there are people all over the place! Space is very limited, so a lot of people live in apartment buildings instead of houses. Those people may have to climb flights of stairs or take an elevator to get to their home. They may not have a yard. With such little space, it is very hard to have a pet. The Big Apple is also noisy, from loud crowds to honking horns to the sirens of police cars. All of the traffic creates a lot of pollution and traffic jams. It can take a long time when traveling by car or bus. Many adults travel for close to an hour each way to go to work. In addition, there is a high crime rate in the city. Oftentimes you will see homeless people in New York City. It is sad to know that some people have nowhere to live. Despite the negative points of the Big Apple, it's a great place to live if you like to always be on the go.

In conclusion, New York City is full of excitement. It truly is the city that never sleeps. You can always stay busy and on the move. There are so many things to see and so many places to go. There are many cities in the United States, but there is no better place to live than the Big Apple.

The Rewards of Recycling

written by Luke See

Have you ever thought about recycling? Do you make sure not to throw plastic bottles in the trash? Maybe your family recycles at home. If not, you should think about trying it. Some people think recycling is not worth their time, but this could not be further from the truth. Recycling is very important because it protects the environment, grows the economy, and builds communities.

First, recycling protects the environment. It does this in many ways. Items that you recycle do not end up in landfills. Landfills are always getting bigger and taking up more space. Throwing recyclable items into landfills is a mistake. Expanding landfills destroy land that could be used for other things. Also, harmful chemicals and gases are released from garbage that is left in landfills. By recycling, you can reduce this garbage.

Additionally, recycling reduces the need for new products to be made. In turn, minerals and forests can be saved. If a company needs to make millions of sheets of paper, its workers must cut down trees to produce that paper. However, if enough people recycle their paper, it can be broken down and made into new products. This saves trees. In this case, recycling is not just saving resources but also protecting nature. Forests are always under threat from businesses that want their resources. These habitats are home to millions of species of plants and animals. They could be lost forever just so companies can harvest resources. Recycling reduces the need for new resources.

The recycling industry is great for the economy as well. Recycling materials protects the environment, but it is also good business. Businesses that rely on recycling do not need new materials. Cutting down a forest or mining for minerals is more expensive than using recycled materials. Companies that use recycled resources are in a good position because their material supplies will not run out as long as people keep recycling. Recycling is the future, as there are only so many nonrenewable resources to be had.

Recycling also creates jobs that can last a long time. This is because the industry is growing larger every day. The recycling industry employs more than 1 million people in the United States. In comparison, garbage companies employ about 250,000 people. Recycling also creates different types of jobs. Some of these include manufacturing jobs for companies that create recycling equipment, as well as labor jobs for people who collect and process recyclables. Recycling even creates retail jobs. The whole recycling industry helps the economy.

Finally, recycling helps build communities. It does this via some of the ways that have already been mentioned. Reducing landfills preserves land for parks, homes, and new stores. Opening new recycling plants creates jobs as well. The recycling industry can also bring people together through community service. You can do this yourself by donating unwanted items. Many charities and community groups raise money by recycling items and selling items for reuse. The next time you think about simply throwing something away, think about the people who could use it elsewhere in the world.

Other community service projects focus on recycling as well. Many towns have highway adoption programs in which people pledge to clean up litter. These programs are beneficial in that people make roadways more attractive while also gathering recyclable materials. By focusing on giving back to your community, you can also protect the environment. This might seem like a small step, but every little bit helps.

In conclusion, recycling and reusing have a positive impact on many aspects of life. These efforts protect and support the environment in a time when it is constantly threatened. Recycling and reusing also benefit companies and people economically. Both processes are acts of community service that help those around you and better the place in which you live.

Works Cited

"Recycling Industry Can Boost the European Economy." *European Environment Agency*, 15 July 2016, www.eea.europa.eu/highlights/recycling-industry-can-boost-the. Accessed 25 April 2018.

United States, Congress, "Recycling: A Component of Strong Community Development." *Recycling: A Component of Strong Community Development*, EPA, 2016.

United States, Congress, Recycling Economic Information. "2016 Recycling Economic Information Report." *2016 Recycling Economic Information Report*, EPA, 2016.

"Why Is Recycling Important?" *UAF Office of Sustainability*, 6 Dec. 2017, www.uaf.edu/sustainability/recycling-program/why-recycle/index.xml. Accessed 25 April 2018.

The History of Numbers

written by Megan Weinman
illustrated by Dion Williams

Imagine a world in which there are no numbers. What if you could not tell the difference between one and two, between ten and twelve, or between one hundred and one thousand? Our lives would be very different. How would you know your age? How would you know what time it was? How would you know the date or year? People need to be able to use numbers and count as part of daily life. Think about how many times you have used a number or counted just today. Knowing the history of numbers and number systems is very important. It will help you understand the world in which you live.

The most amazing thing about the number system most commonly used today is just how common it really is. The same kinds of numbers and systems are used by most of the modern world. We speak many different languages and use different types of writing. However, very few number systems are used. This is especially true in science where just one number system is used. It is the system many of us have used since childhood. This system is made up of the ten symbols one, two, three, four, five, six, seven, eight, nine, and zero. These ten symbols are used to show all other numbers. This system is one you have used for years.

There are two important things to remember about numbers. First, there are names given to numbers. Second, there are symbols that stand for numbers. Both of these ideas will help you understand numbers and how the number systems used today came to be.

Before the spoken and written number order, the number words, and the number symbols came to be, there was another way people shared the meaning of numbers. Can you guess what it was? People used gestures to show numbers. Using all ten fingers, people could show many different numbers. We often still use our fingers for small numbers. Imagine trying to

show the number nine thousand, nine hundred ninety-nine using just your ten fingers! There is proof found in early letters and printed books that fingers were used to show very large numbers up to nine thousand, nine hundred ninety-nine! The word *digit* even comes from the Latin word for finger, *digitus*. It is not known exactly where "finger numbers" came from and when they came to be. They were likely invented by people making business transactions. The finger numbers were useful in business even when the traders did not speak the same language. Finger numbers are not as commonly used today. One place that finger gestures are still used to show numbers is in the stock exchange.

Finger gestures are a form of silent communication. They are not good enough for keeping lasting records. The same is true for the spoken number word. It is not useful unless someone remembers it. Numbers need to be written down or stored in an easy way in order to last. Today, we use computers to store numbers. Ancient man also invented processes for storing numbers. For example, ancient man used sticks to count coconuts. Each stick stood for one coconut. Another old counting process used pebbles to count soldiers. A pebble was dropped into a box each time a soldier passed by. Once ten pebbles were in the box, they were taken out. One pebble was placed in a second box. When there were ten pebbles in the second box, those ten were taken out. One pebble was placed into a third box. This continued until all soldiers passed. The pebbles could then easily be counted. A different value was given to a pebble based on which box it was placed in. A third way of counting was used by the Egyptians. They used a simple stroke to show one and six symbols to show ten, one hundred, one thousand, ten thousand, one hundred thousand, and one million. These symbols could each be repeated up to nine times. This was a tallying system. The Romans also used a tallying system. They added the amounts of five, fifty, and five hundred to their system. This let the Romans use fewer symbols, and it created numbers that were easier to read. Other systems were created that did not include repeating symbols. The Greek number system used the letters of the alphabet as number signs. Each number had its own symbol and its own value. This took away the repetition of symbols and made numbers shorter and easier to read. Unfortunately, many different symbols were needed. None of these systems alone were ideal. People needed a better number system with a small number of symbols that repeated a pattern.

The Hindu-Arabic number system has all of the best parts of the early number systems. It uses symbols for the numbers zero to nine and repeats these symbols often. No tallying is needed. Beginning with ten, the meaning of each symbol depends on where it is in the number. It is a base ten system. This means the units are multiples of ten. The symbol two could be used to stand for two, twenty, two hundred, or two thousand. Where the symbol two is in the number changes the value of the symbol. In this system, a number can be written down no matter how long it is. There is a big difference between this system and the Roman numeral system. The symbol zero is used as a place holder. For example, a zero is put in the tens place if there are no tens units. You must write something to stand for nothing! The symbol zero is very important in the Hindu-Arabic number system. However, zero was not even seen as a "real" number until the seventeenth century.

In terms of how number systems have formed over the years, it is clear that numbers, science, and technology have grown together. The question "Why does this happen?" turned into "How does this happen?" This meant that amounts were needed. New types of mathematics began to develop. The growth of numbers and number systems made the technology used today possible. Without the earliest simple number systems, more complicated number systems could not exist. The finger gestures, spoken number words, and written number words from long ago were used to make the math number system people know and use today.

Amazing National Parks: Volcanoes and Mountains

written by Jill Fisher
illustrated by Dion Williams

There are nearly sixty national parks in the United States. The US government cares for these areas. The government has written many special laws to help. These laws keep the land safe. They guard the animals that live there. The national parks are known for many reasons. They have incredible wildlife and pretty landscapes. They offer a range of outdoor activities. Millions of tourists visit them each year. They come from all parts of the world. Two of the most popular parks to see are Hawaii Volcanoes and Rocky Mountain National Parks. This splendid pair has many similarities and differences.

Hawaii Volcanoes and Rocky Mountain National Parks are similar in many ways. Both are open every day of the year. They became national parks in the early 1900s. Each has a gorgeous view. They offer a variety of fun activities, like hiking and horseback riding. Each place is perfect to relax. They are also both known for their unpredictable weather. Either place can be cold and rainy on any given day. It is best to wear layers of clothing. This way you are ready for all weather. Both of these parks are partly created with igneous rock. Igneous rock forms when hot lava cools.

These two parks also have key differences. One is a group of volcanoes. The other is a mountain range. They are found in very different locations. Hawaii Volcanoes stands on the southern part of Hawaii, also known as the Big Island. There you will find two of the world's most active volcanoes. Rocky Mountain National Park is in northern Colorado. It is one of the longest mountain ranges in the world. The parks were shaped in different ways. Over millions of years the lava from the volcanoes formed the shape of the Hawaiian island. The Rocky Mountains were slowly shaped by glaciers and rivers. Hawaii Volcanoes has less extreme weather than Rocky Mountain National Park. In Hawaii Volcanoes, the temperature stays between fifty and seventy degrees for most of the year. At Rocky Mountain, it can range from below zero to the upper eighties. The animals found at each park are quite different. Hawaii is home to many rare birds. You may also see an endangered sea turtle. In the Rocky Mountains, many animals have thick fur. They need it to keep warm in the cold weather. Some examples are elks, moose, bears, and bighorn sheep.

Hawaii Volcanoes and Rocky Mountain National Parks have many similarities. They also have many differences. Yet each is a treasure in its own way. It is important to care for the national parks. In doing so, the natural beauty of the land will be saved. The animals will be protected. Plants, animals, and rock forms will remain for future generations to enjoy them. Whether you'd like to view an active volcano or climb a mountain, everyone can agree that the sights at both of these parks are out of this world.

Nurturing Nature: The Life of Rachel Carson

written by Michael Scotto
illustrated by David Rushbrook

Rachel Carson held many titles. She was an ecologist. That is, she studied how living things relate to nature. She worked as a scientist. She was a famous author. Most impressive is how she used her many skills. Her writing joined a love of nature with a strong knowledge of science. It inspired the people. It even moved the president of the United States. Carson is known as the mother of the environmental movement. This movement began in the 1960s and lives on today.

Rachel Louise Carson was born on May 27, 1907. She grew up in Springdale, Pennsylvania. That is a small river town north of Pittsburgh. The Carson family was quite poor. They lived in a tiny, cramped farmhouse. However, around their farmhouse was a massive stretch of land. It spanned over sixty-five acres—the size of forty-nine football fields! The land was full of beautiful sights, plant life, and wild animals.

As a girl, Carson spent a lot of time outdoors. She collected the fossils of sea animals. She dug them from the bed of the Allegheny River. She learned about nature with her mother. They often went bird watching together. Carson loved to learn how different kinds of creatures lived. Only one thing interested her more: writing.

Rachel Carson began to write stories at a very young age. Her mother was very encouraging. Carson's first stories were about woodland animals. Her characters were birds and mice. After a few years, Carson published a story in *St. Nicholas*. It was the best-known children's magazine of the time. At the mere age of eleven, she had become a published writer!

For the rest of her childhood, Carson's dream was to write for a living. She published more stories in *St.*

Nicholas. In a single year, the magazine printed three of her works. *St. Nicholas* awarded her a special cash prize for being published so often. By age fourteen, Carson was being paid a penny a word for her writing. After high school, she moved to Pittsburgh to pursue a degree in English. She signed up at the Pennsylvania College for Women, or PCW.

Carson almost did not make it to college. She had earned a scholarship. Sadly, it did not cover the whole cost. Carson's parents could not afford to help pay the rest. Luckily, the president of PCW saw great promise in the young woman. She asked friends to help pay Carson's tuition. Through their kindness, Carson was able to begin her studies.

Carson did wonderfully in her first year. She earned excellent grades. She also published a short story in the school magazine. She seemed well on her way to becoming a professional writer. Then the unexpected happened. Between Carson's first and second year, PCW changed its rules to graduate. All students now had to take two semesters of science. Carson signed up to take biology. She did not know it then, but this single class would change the path of her life forever.

Carson's biology teacher was Mary Scott Skinker. She was tough, but she always tried to help her students. She also set a strong example. Skinker was a woman who had made a career in science. That was a rare sight at the time. Her teacher's drive and success reminded Carson of how much she had loved learning about nature with her mother. It made the young woman rethink her chosen path. Was her calling really to be a novelist? Or could she become a scientist herself? She decided to find out. After that year, Rachel Carson changed her focus from English to science.

Many challenges followed the change. The biggest involved Mary Skinker. She had become more than a teacher. She was a mentor and friend. Soon, though, Skinker left PCW. She moved to Baltimore to study at Johns Hopkins University. She wished to earn her doctoral degree. Her move forced Carson to learn on

her own. She worked in the science lab with little help. Even so, in 1928, Carson graduated with honors.

Carson decided to follow Mary Skinker to Johns Hopkins. She wished to pursue a master's degree in biology. Skinker helped her to get a full scholarship. She also helped Carson find a summer job at a science lab. It was called the Marine Biological Laboratory, or MBL. It was located in Woods Hole, Massachusetts. Its specialty was the study of water animals and their environment.

Carson's summer at MBL was one of the best of her life. The lab had many resources. It was also one of only a few labs that treated women and men as equals. Carson learned skills that she had not been able to pick up on her own. She met world-famous scientists. The ones she liked most worked for the United States government. Carson grew excited to start her graduate studies.

In graduate school, Carson faced more struggles. Some involved her coursework. Classes were much harder than they had been at PCW. It was tough to achieve the same level of success that she had before. Still, Carson managed to earn her master's degree in 1932. She rushed on to pursue her doctorate, like her friend Mary Skinker.

Other problems were personal. These were more serious. Carson's family farm in Springdale had been overtaken by factories and cheap housing. The land had been ruined. This hurt Carson deeply. Her whole family came to live with her in Baltimore. Soon, the strain of supporting everyone became too much. Carson had to drop out of school.

It was a dark time for Carson. She feared that her dream of being a scientist was over. Her family had to come first. To help earn money, she dug up some stories she had written years before. She aimed to sell them to magazines. When Carson read the stories, it awoke her love for writing once again. At the same time, Mary Skinker came to Carson's aid. She helped her friend find a job working for the US government.

At the time, science jobs were scarce. But the Bureau of Fisheries did not need a scientist. It needed a writer. The bureau wanted to create a series of radio programs. The programs would educate the public about its work to protect the oceans and rivers. This project had turned out to be quite a pain. Trained writers could not describe the science of conservation. The scientists could not write well. But for Carson, the project was a perfect union of her two loves. Her work proved to be a hit. In the summer of 1936, the bureau offered her a permanent job as a scientist.

Carson took the job. She also kept writing. She wrote articles about marine science for the *Baltimore Sun* newspaper. Then she got her big break. *The Atlantic Monthly* bought one of her essays! This magazine was read by tens of thousands. A popular publisher read her work and offered her a book contract. By November of 1941, Carson had finished the book and it was published.

Carson's first book was *Under the Sea-Wind*. It told the stories of sea animals and how they lived. Critics adored its mix of poetic writing and detailed science. The public did not take much notice. How could it? Shortly after the book came out, the Japanese attacked Pearl Harbor. Overnight, the country was at war. There was not much interest in the lives of sea animals. Yet Carson was not discouraged. All through World War II, she published stories in *Collier's* and *Reader's Digest*.

Not everything Carson wrote was accepted, though. In 1945, she learned about a chemical called DDT. It was invented to help farmers kill pests. However, it also killed helpful insects, like bees and grasshoppers. It could even kill birds and other small animals. Carson read many reports of its dangers. She offered to write about it for *Reader's Digest*. The editor turned her down.

After the war ended, Carson began a new book. She got an agent to help sell it. Her agent also became a good friend. Tragically, as Carson made one new friend, she lost an old one. In 1947, Mary Scott Skinker died of cancer. Carson stayed at her bedside until she passed.

After her friend's death, Carson continued work on her book. It took years to finish, but it was time well spent. In 1951, *The Sea Around Us* was published. This time the book caught the imagination of both critics and readers alike. It spent eighty-six weeks on the *New York Times* Best Seller list. For thirty-nine of those weeks, it was number one. It was printed in thirty different languages. It even won the National Book Award. *The Sea Around Us* made Rachel Carson a household name. In 1952, she left her government job to write full-time.

Carson moved with her mother back to Woods Hole, Massachusetts. Near the lab where she had held her first job, the famed author began her next book. By 1955, Carson's *The Edge of the Sea* was complete. It was a top-ten bestseller for nearly half a year. Carson had ideas for many future projects. However, her personal life pushed writing into the background. In 1956, one of Carson's nieces passed away. She adopted her niece's son. Also, her mother's health had begun to fail. Carson spent a great time caring for her at Woods Hole and at her summer home in Maine. In the fall of 1958, Carson's mother died of pneumonia.

Rachel Carson's mother had inspired her love of both nature and writing. Her death was a crushing loss. Carson might have given up her work if not for a letter that she had received. A Massachusetts woman had written to Carson some months back. The woman owned a sanctuary, or protected area of land, for birds. One day, she had come home to a horrible sight: all of the birds in her sanctuary had dropped dead. They died only days after the government had sprayed the area with DDT.

Just like that, Carson had found the subject for her next book. She had been concerned about DDT for years. More broadly, she worried about the effects of technology and pollution on wildlife. She had seen the smoky skies of industrial Pittsburgh. She had watched her childhood home be destroyed by factories. She could even see the effects near her home in Maine. Carson had to act. She researched the dangers of pesticides. She studied their threat to humans and to animals, like songbirds. The image of dying songbirds inspired the book's title: *Silent Spring*.

In 1962, *Silent Spring* took the world by storm. The book showed how dangerous it was to use pesticides carelessly. Carson thought they could be useful, but that they needed to be used with more caution. She saw how all living things affected one another. Humans were part of a complex world. When they hurt nature, they also hurt themselves.

There was a range of reactions to *Silent Spring*. Chemical companies hated the book. They attacked Carson however they could. Some slammed her research. They threatened to sue her for spreading false information. Some attacked her as a person, saying a female scientist could not be taken seriously. Others read her work and felt great concern for nature. One of these people was President John F. Kennedy. After reading Carson's work, he formed a special task force. Its job was to advise him on the environment.

President Kennedy's group sided with Carson. The US Senate began to look into the dangers of pesticides. *Silent Spring* had started to effect real change. Sadly, its writer did not get to see the results. While writing the book, Carson had learned that she had cancer. Her health worsened as the book was published. On April 14, 1964, Rachel Carson passed away at only fifty-six years old.

Though Carson's journey was over, *Silent Spring* kept on going. Congress passed the first laws protecting food, water, and air from toxins. In 1970, President Richard Nixon created the Environmental Protection Agency, or EPA. That same year, the United States celebrated its first Earth Day. Only two years after that, DDT was banned in the United States. What started as a book had grown into a movement.

In 1980, Carson was honored with the highest award a civilian can earn: the Presidential Medal of Freedom. Later, the city of Pittsburgh named a bridge for her. It crosses the Allegheny River, which runs all the way past her childhood home. A hiking trail along that river also bears her name. *TIME* magazine called Rachel Carson "one of the most influential people of the 20th century." She remains a hero to activists, scientists, and everyday lovers of nature. With her pen and her passion, she changed the world.

Ruby Bridges: A Brave Girl Who Changed History

written by Jennifer Tkocs
illustrated by William McCoy III

The word "segregation" describes setting people or things apart. For a very long time, governments and businesses in the United States of America segregated people by the color of their skin. This was true at restaurants, on buses, and even at schools. African Americans suffered most due to segregation. Segregation was enforced across the country, and the city of New Orleans, Louisiana, was no exception. However, in 1960, segregation in the schools of New Orleans changed forever. It happened because one brave little girl, Ruby Bridges, walked into William Frantz Elementary School. Her actions ignited the end of segregation in schools in her city.

Ruby Bridges was born in 1954 in Tylertown, Mississippi. She lived on a farm with her parents and grandparents. Her parents did not have very much money. They thought moving to a bigger city might give them a better life. The Bridges family moved to New Orleans when Ruby was four years old.

The Supreme Court had ruled in 1954 that school segregation was unconstitutional, or illegal. In 1960, though, New Orleans schools were still segregated. Black students and white students had to go to separate schools. Ruby attended an all-black kindergarten.

Things changed when Ruby was ready to enter first grade. The New Orleans school system made a test for incoming black students. This test was meant to determine if the children were eligible to attend an all-white school. The test-makers deliberately wrote the exam to be very hard. They hoped it would keep segregation alive in New Orleans schools.

At first, Ruby's parents disagreed whether or not she should take the test. Her father was afraid of what might happen if Ruby went to an all-white school. Her mother, though, thought Ruby would get a better education there. They agreed to let Ruby take the test.

Ruby Bridges was very bright. She passed the test easily, even though it was very hard. Only she and five other African American children passed the test. Ruby used to have to walk a very long distance to attend the closest all-black school. Now, though, she could walk just a short distance and attend the all-white school near her home.

But things were not easy for Ruby. The government stalled on integrating the all-white school. This meant that she had to begin the school year at her old school. Finally, on November 14, 1960, Ruby was able to attend classes at her new school for the first time.

– 114 –

Many were concerned that people who supported segregation would cause problems at the school. Because of this, a judge ordered federal marshals to escort Ruby inside. This was a good idea. On Ruby's first day, many people stood outside to protest her arrival. They shouted and threw things at Ruby. The marshals protected her. Still, the chaos meant no classes could be held that day.

Ruby faced prejudice for a long time at her new school. Many white parents pulled their children out of school entirely. Ruby stayed in a single classroom by herself each day with her teacher, Mrs. Henry. Her family received threats. Her father lost his job.

Each day, though, Ruby showed up to school. Federal marshals stayed by her side. She worked hard on her lessons with Mrs. Henry. Her family still faced discrimination from many white families in their town. However, Ruby's family also began to receive notes and words of support. Some families supported integration. They helped Ruby's family by babysitting. They also found a job for her father.

Over time, the chaos calmed down. Parents brought their children back to the school. By the second year, more black students came to William Frantz. Ruby's classroom included both black and white children. She attended fully integrated schools for the rest of her time as a student.

Ruby Bridges still works to end prejudice and discrimination. She went back to the very school where her journey began to serve as a parent-community liaison. Her goal is to help end prejudice by engaging with parents. When William Frantz Elementary faced budget crises and, later, extreme water damage from Hurricane Katrina, Ruby Bridges helped raise money for the school. It has since been renovated. It reopened as a charter school, Akili Academy. Ruby Bridges still visits the students there to share her story.

Works Cited

"Biography for Kids: Ruby Bridges." *Ducksters*, www.ducksters.com/history/civil_rights/ruby_bridges.php. Accessed 15 Feb. 2017.

"Ruby Bridges Bio." *Biography.com*, www.biography.com/people/rubybridges-475426. Accessed 15 Feb. 2017.

Weible, David Robert. "New Life for the School Where Ruby Bridges Made History." *The Huffington Post*, 13 May 2014, www.huffingtonpost.com/national-trust-for-historic-preservation/new-lifefor-the-school-w_b_4956789.html. Accessed 15 Feb. 2017.

Thump in the Night

written by Vincent J. Scotto

Theodore flew down the mountainside in a flash. He soared through the air like a bird, but he had no wings. Just as he approached the ground, Theodore began to level out, but he landed in a bed of flowers with a loud thump.

THUMP! THUMP!

Theodore woke up from a deep slumber to find that he was on the floor next to his bed. It was just a dream, but it felt real enough to him. After all, he did fall out of his bed and hit the floor hard.

THUMP! THUMP!

Theodore heard the noise, but it was not him this time. It was something else entirely. He got up off the floor and cracked his bedroom door open. He peeked out into the hallway, but he did not see anything unusual.

"Maybe I just hit my head and my ears are still ringing," Theodore said quietly to himself. Without a second thought, Theodore closed his bedroom door. He walked back to his bed.

THUMP! THUMP!

Now he was certain he had heard something. Theodore went back to the hallway and crept to his parents' room. The door creaked as he opened it. He peered inside, but neither of his parents was there.

"Mom?" Theodore whispered. "Dad?" Neither parent returned an answer. "Did you hear that noise?"

THUMP! THUMP!

Startled, Theodore determined that the ominous noise had come from somewhere on the floor below. He slinked down the hallway and toward the spiral staircase. He leaned over the side to look down, but he did not see anything except for a flashing light.

"Dad?" he whispered. "Is that you down there?" No answer.

THUMP! THUMP!

Theodore wiped the glistening sweat off his brow and skulked down the steps to avoid making any noise. He looked out into the kitchen first, but he could not see anything. He peered into the living room next. The television set was on, but it was just flashing white snow; it made no sound. Theodore thought that was unusual.

THUMP! THUMP!

The noise got louder. Theodore thought that he must be close to the origin of the sound. He still could not quite decipher where it was coming from, but it sounded like it might be in the basement. Theodore avoided the basement most of the time, especially at night.

"Mom!" he called into the house, much louder than before. "Dad!" Still, he received no reply. He heard nothing except for the sound of the pounding down below.

Theodore grabbed his baseball bat, which was lying on the floor in the living room. His mother always told him to put his things away, but this time, it helped that the bat was not stowed away in his closet upstairs. He headed toward the basement door, ready for anything. He cracked open the door and peered down the steps. He could not see a thing. He flipped the light switch, but no light came from the bulb below.

THUMP! THUMP!

The pounding was louder than ever. Theodore dripped with sweat as he tiptoed down the basement stairs. Each step creaked beneath his feet, but he was too far into his investigation to turn back. He gripped the bat tighter as he approached the bottom of the stairs. As he reached his foot out to touch the floor, he stepped on something prickly and fell to the ground with a crash. The bat flew out of his hand and into the dark chamber. Unable to see anything at all at this point, he reached around for the bat to no avail.

THUMP! THUMP!

"Mom!" he yelled in hopes that she might finally answer.

"Are you all right, Theodore?" his mother's voice called. She flipped the light switch. Theodore looked up from the floor. He was back in his bedroom. He was dripping with sweat.

"Did you have a bad dream?" she asked. Theodore wiped his face and stood up.

"I…guess that's what happened," he replied, a bit confused.

"I think you need to stop watching those scary movies," she scolded. "They are obviously affecting how you sleep."

"All right, Mom."

Theodore climbed back into his bed and pulled up the covers.

"Goodnight, Theo."

"Goodnight, Mom."

Theodore's mother turned off the light and closed his bedroom door. He took a deep breath and let it out. He was relieved that it was all just a dream. He rolled over, pulled the covers tight, and closed his eyes. Just as he was about to fall back to sleep, Theodore's bed began to quake.

THUMP! THUMP!

Amelia Earhart

written by Jennifer Tkocs
illustrated by David Rushbrook

Amelia Earhart was born in Kansas on July 24, 1897. She was always very curious. Amelia's parents helped her and her sister try many new things.

In Amelia's time, many jobs were held mostly by men. Amelia wanted one of those jobs. She read stories about women who were lawyers, engineers, and movie directors.

Soon, Amelia finished with school. She became a nurse. She worked in Canada during World War I.

Amelia's life changed forever in 1920. She was visiting family in California. She went to an air show. That is a show where pilots do tricks with their planes. She met a pilot named Frank Hawkes. For ten dollars, Amelia got a ride in Frank's plane.

Right away, Amelia knew she was meant to fly. She took flying lessons. She worked hard and saved her money. In less than a year, she bought her own plane.

Soon, Amelia set her first flying record. She flew her plane fourteen thousand feet in the air. She was the first woman to do this. She set another record in 1928. Amelia and two male pilots flew from America to England. She was the first female pilot to cross the Atlantic Ocean.

Amelia took many long flights by herself. In 1932, she flew across the Atlantic again. This time she went alone. She was the first woman to fly across the Atlantic by herself. The weather was icy and windy, but she made a good landing.

In 1935, she flew alone across the Pacific Ocean. She was the first person to do that. She earned many awards and medals. One medal even came from the president.

In 1937, Amelia and her navigator, Fred Noonan, began her longest journey. They planned to fly all the way around the world. Amelia wanted one last great flight.

They only made it most of the way. With just seven thousand miles left, they fell out of contact.

The Navy and Coast Guard searched and searched. But they never found Amelia or her plane. There have been many rumors about what happened. No one knows the truth.

Amelia Earhart is one of the most famous pilots in history. Her story inspired many, even though the ending may never truly be known.

A Horse and Paul Revere
written by Mark Weimer
illustrated by Sean Kennedy

It was 1774 when Paul Revere **began** to work as an express **rider**. His job was to deliver news, messages, and **papers** to northern cities in the colonies. He was **based** in Boston. He rode by horseback to cities as far as Philadelphia. It was important that he could travel at a fast **pace**. He was very good at his job.

By the spring of 1775, British **rule** over the American colonies had become very shaky. The British had forced taxes on the colonies that colonists felt were wrong. In 1768, British troops were sent to force payment of those taxes. This was something that Revere and other colonists did not like. In 1770, colonists began to riot in Boston. British soldiers shot at them, killing several. After this **event**, tensions **rose** even higher. Revere became even angrier and **sided** with the colonists. Colonists met secretly to talk about the plan to break away from the British and become independent. Revere joined an organization called the Sons of Liberty. People began to feel that war was coming. Revere feared that he might be captured by the British army. To avoid this, he told other spies for the Sons of Liberty to hang lanterns in the bell tower of a church in Boston. Hanging one lantern meant that the British troops were marching by land. Two hanging lanterns meant that the troops were crossing Boston Harbor first and then marching.

The next week, Revere was told to ride quickly to Lexington, Massachusetts. He needed to find two men: Samuel Adams and John Hancock. His job was to warn them that the British were on their way to arrest them. Looking at the church, he saw two lanterns. That meant that the British were crossing the harbor first and then marching. It takes an army time to load into

boats. This gave Revere a head start. Two peers helped Revere across the harbor to Charlestown. There, he was given a horse. He **laced** up his boots and **rode** out of Charlestown at 11:00 p.m.

Revere began his **ride** well ahead of the British. Along the way, he **bravely** warned the houses that he passed. He shouted in a loud **tone**, "The British are coming!" He **made** his way north, meeting two other riders along the way. At one point, all three were captured by a British patrol. The two other riders escaped almost immediately. However, Revere was held for a longer **time**. Soon, he was released without a horse. Revere still went to Lexington and helped Hancock and Adams. The other two riders **rode** on to Concord to prepare an armed defense. Shortly after Adams and Hancock fled, the British army arrived, and Revere witnessed the **beginning** of the American Revolutionary War.

Ten-Year-Old Rescues Kitten from Tree

written by Katie Catanzarite

OAKVIEW, MASS.—This past Friday, Sept. 4, 2015, Isaac Jonas, 10, rescued a kitten from a tree on his way home from school. Jonas is a fourth grade student at Oakview Elementary. He was walking to his house on Walnut Street when the incident occurred. He claims to have heard an animal crying. When he looked up, he saw the tabby kitten perched on a mulberry tree branch. Jonas was able to climb the trunk and use his jacket to catch the kitten.

The Oakview Observer spoke with Jonas and his mother, Lisa Jonas. It turns out that the boy is no stranger to acrobatics.

"He's always been fearless," Ms. Jonas, 36, said. "He's been climbing the trees in our backyard since he could walk!"

Jonas himself bashfully admits to his antics. He expressed that he was just trying to help his elderly neighbor. He had decided to help the kitten when he recognized that the kitten belonged to Hazel Shelly, who lives next door to the Jonases.

"I wasn't really scared of falling," Jonas said. "I climb trees all the time. I just didn't want Mrs. Shelly's cat to get hurt. She only brought him home this week."

The Observer also caught up with Shelly, 72. She proudly brought out her kitten and showed off the little daredevil. Shelly stated that the kitten had escaped from her house when she was out getting the mail. She had walked around the block and hoped to catch sight of him. Because the kitten is still so small and Shelly is unable to walk very far, she could not locate him. Shelly was worried that the animal would be hit by a car. It was not until Jonas showed up at her doorstep that she could finally relax.

"Isaac had the poor thing wrapped up in his jacket!" Shelly said. "I'm just so glad neither of them got hurt."

In gratitude toward Jonas, Shelly has allowed him to name the kitten. Most appropriately, Jonas has decided to call the animal "Trouble."

News spread around Oakview Elementary about Jonas's bravery. At that point, the school's principal, Dr. Robert Stanton, contacted *The Observer* with this heartwarming story.

"Isaac is a top student, and he's always willing to help out his friends—even the furry ones," Stanton said. Stanton is currently trying to raise animal life awareness at the elementary school. Stanton is hosting a presentation from volunteers at the Oakview Humane Society next week.

No matter how big, small, old, or young, there are always people like Isaac Jonas who are willing to help others. It is a lesson that the Oakview community can hold close to its heart. From now on, take a lesson from Jonas: Always be willing to help your friends—even the furry ones.

The Constitution of the United States

written by Vincent J. Scotto

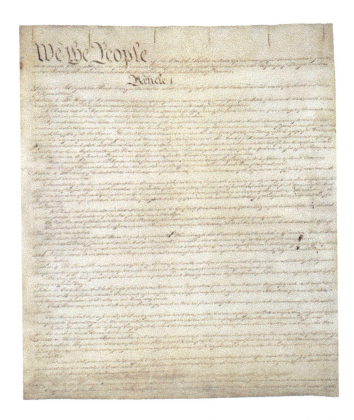

The Constitution of the United States of America was not yet written when the 13 colonies declared their independence. In fact, the New World was not quite ready to be a nation for several years. Several key events had to occur before the colonies could accept the Constitution.

The 13 colonies became states after the Declaration of Independence was written in 1776. The states were not completely united, however. They had not yet designed a central government. In the beginning, the young land mostly focused on fighting the British. During the war, the states designed a central government that followed a set of laws called the Articles of Confederation.

The people still worried about a strong central government. When leaders approved the Articles of Confederation in 1781, they created a weak central government. It had little control over the states. Representatives of different states often argued. There was no branch of federal government to enforce the laws. The nation also had no judicial branch. Since there was no tax and each state had its own currency, there was no national economy. Thus, foreign and interstate trade was very complicated and messy. Some states had their own militaries, but none of them would volunteer to create a national force. The weakness of the Articles of Confederation made it very difficult for the states to remain a nation.

Many recognized the weakness of the Articles of Confederation. In 1786, representatives from nearly half of the states began promoting a convention. The convention was a gathering to create new rules and regulations. The first states that joined the convention did so to address economic issues. However, when more states grew interested, leaders turned the gathering into the Constitutional Convention. The goal now was to revise the Articles of Confederation. Some believed that they would merely revise the existing Articles. A few men, however, set out to do something entirely new.

At the start of the convention in May 1787, George Washington, a respected general during the American Revolution, was immediately named the convention's president. Twelve of the states sent delegates, or representatives. Only Rhode Island did not participate. Rhode Island had no interest in creating a stronger central government. The delegates from the other states quickly determined that they needed to start fresh. They first proposed that the government should consist of three branches: legislative, executive, and judicial. With that, the process of creating the Constitution began.

Several ideas made the Constitution stronger than the Articles of Confederation. Unlike the Articles, the Constitution called for two sections of representation from each state. The legislative branch would represent each state by population size in one section. It would represent each state equally in the other section. These two sections eventually became known as the House of Representatives and the Senate. In addition, the delegates created a legislative branch to make laws.

The delegates also created an executive branch, which was to be led by a president. This branch existed to enforce the laws. Enforcing laws was very important but also controversial. When the states learned about the planned presidency, they worried that it would be no different from having a king. Finally, the delegates created a judicial branch, which was to be headed by a Supreme Court. The judicial branch was created to explain the laws. Its appointees would also decide whether court cases followed the laws in the Constitution.

When the drafted Constitution was sent to the states, each state demanded changes. Many feared losing their rights to a central government, like they would under the rule of a king. Many demands for changes involved gaining protection from the government itself. With help from a committee, James Madison wrote 10 amendments to the Constitution.

These became known as the Bill of Rights. After several months, the convention delegates met again to adopt and sign the Constitution. Only three of the 41 members voted against it.

After the delegates signed the Constitution in September 1787, the states still needed to ratify it. Delaware was the first state to do this. It took some time for other states to follow Delaware's lead. The Constitution became law when the ninth state, New Hampshire, ratified it in June 1788, almost a year later. Still worried about a strong central government, Rhode Island representatives took another two years to ratify the Constitution. After gaining Rhode Island's approval in 1790, all 13 states became the United States of America.

The Constitution has stood for more than 200 years. Over the years, additional adjustments have been made to the Constitution to improve the nation. Still, the Constitution and its first 10 amendments remain a central part of the way laws are created, enforced, and judged in the United States. The events leading up to the Constitution's creation were challenging, but those challenges ultimately led to one of the freest nations in the world to have a strong central government.

Works Cited

"Branches of Government." *USA.gov*, www.usa.gov/branches-of-government. Accessed 11 Feb. 2017.

"Constitutional Convention and Ratification, 1787–1789." *U.S. Department of State - Office of the Historian*, history. state.gov/milestones/1784-1800/convention-and-ratification. Accessed 11 Feb. 2017.

"Constitutional Convention Convenes in Philadelphia." *History.com*, www.history.com/this-day-in-history/ constitutional-convention-convenes-in-philadelphia. Accessed 11 Feb. 2017.

"Judicial Branch: The Supreme Court." *Congressforkids.net*, www.congressforkids.net/Judicialbranch_ supremecourt.htm. Accessed 11 Feb. 2017.

"The Thirteen Colonies." *History.com*, http://www.history.com/topics/thirteen-colonies. Accessed 11 Feb. 2017.

Researching Made Simple

written by Vincent J. Scotto

The task of writing a research report can be challenging. A great report requires a variety of resources. Using different resources makes your report more reliable. Finding a variety of resources is easy; you can use many different kinds.

You can use print books as resources for a research report. Print books are popular resources that are easy to use. They offer a variety of information. You can easily handle them and flip between pages quickly. You can buy books for long-term use, or you can check them out at a library if you only need them for a while.

You can also use an encyclopedia as a resource for a research report. An encyclopedia contains general information or facts about a specific subject. In an encyclopedia, it is common for many experts to contribute to a topic. The passages are usually much shorter than those found in books. This can make it easier to find information for a research report.

Academic journals are yet another type of resource that you can use for a research report. They are very accessible and even easier to use. Also, they are published more frequently than books. Academic journals usually contain the most up-to-date research. They include information about prior research, new research, history, and current theories. You can find academic journals either in libraries or on the Internet.

Print books, encyclopedias, and academic journals are just a few resources that you can reference when writing a research report. There are plenty more resources beyond these three. Using a variety of resources to write a report is easy. There are so many resources from which to choose. However, if you only use books, encyclopedias, and academic journals, you would still have more than enough resources to write a great research report. The only thing you would need to do is start searching for the right information. It does not get much easier than that.

Igneous Rock (First Hook)

written by Vincent Scotto

Igneous rocks account for 64.7 percent of Earth's crust. They are one of the three main types of rocks covering planet Earth. Igneous rocks form when liquid magma cools. Their composition depends on the cooling process. The process typically happens because of three changes: a change in temperature, a change in pressure, or a change in chemical make-up. Usually, all three changes happen to some degree. Scientists have found over seven hundred unique forms of igneous rocks. Scientists classify these rocks by crystal size and composition. Igneous rocks have smaller minerals when they cool quickly. For example, basalt rocks have tiny minerals. Their minerals can only be seen under a microscope. Igneous rocks have larger minerals when they cool slowly. Granite rocks have minerals large enough to be seen by the naked eye. Igneous rocks can cool in just a few moments during a volcanic eruption. They can also take millions of years to cool beneath Earth's crust.

Igneous Rock (Second Hook)

written by Vincent Scotto

Igneous rocks are the most abundant of the three main types of rocks on Earth's crust. More than seven hundred types of igneous rocks have been found. Igneous rocks start as melted rock, or magma, beneath Earth's surface. Over time, the magma cools and transforms. Some igneous rocks cool rapidly. Others take millions of years to cool. The rate at which the magma cools determines the size of the minerals that compose the rock. For example, magma cools quickly when it erupts from a volcano. It turns solid in the open air or near Earth's surface. Pumice and basalt are examples of volcanic rocks. Both contain tiny minerals. Some of these minerals can only be seen under a microscope. When an igneous rock cools more slowly, it tends to contain larger minerals. Granite is an igneous rock that forms very slowly. It can take thousands or even millions of years to reach a solid state. Each individual mineral in granite is large enough to be seen with the naked eye. The variety in igneous rocks is truly a wonder!

Igneous Rock (Third Hook)

written by Vincent J. Scotto

Did you know that igneous rock gets its name from the Latin word for fire? Igneous rock transforms into rock from liquid hot magma below Earth's crust. Igneous rock is the most abundant of type of rock found in Earth's crust. It comprises almost two-thirds of Earth's crust. Some forms of igneous rock cool quickly into a solid state during a volcanic eruption. Others form over millions of years. The rocks slowly push up from inside Earth toward the surface. The cooling process determines the forms of igneous rock. When the rock cools more quickly, the minerals that comprise it tend to be small. Basalt rocks are a good example. Basalt contains microscopic minerals that can look almost like glass. When igneous rock forms more slowly, its minerals tend to be larger. Granite rocks show this very well. Granite cools beneath Earth's surface. This is the main reason why it takes longer to cool. Some types of igneous rock form so slowly that their mineral clumps can be up to three feet long. This variance in cooling time is the reason there are more than seven hundred identified types of igneous rock. The "fire" rock certainly is a fascinating one!

Ford's Assembly Line

written by Summer York
illustrated by Sean Ricciardi

In the early 1900s, there were few cars on the roads. Cars were difficult and expensive to build. Because of this, only wealthy people could afford to own them. But Henry Ford, who owned the Ford Motor Company, had a different idea. He wanted to build less expensive cars—cars that everyone could afford. In 1908, Ford produced the Model T, a simple vehicle that was cheaper to make. Still, Ford sought a way to lower costs even further.

After much research, Ford and his team created a system called the assembly line. The assembly line followed three main concepts. The first concept involved interchangeable parts. Interchangeable parts are parts that are always made the same way. Before, craftsmen had to make each car part by hand. Interchangeable parts, however, could be made in large numbers. This saved time and cut labor costs.

The second concept behind the assembly line was the division of labor. Ford broke the process of building the Model T into 84 different steps. He trained each worker to do only one step in the process. In the past, workers had to do many different jobs in the plant. Ford's new plan involved each worker becoming an expert in one simple job. This allowed workers to produce the Model T faster.

The third concept behind the assembly line was called continuous flow. Instead of making the workers move around the factory, Ford made the parts move to the workers. He did this using a conveyor belt system.

It moved the parts around the whole factory. The workers stayed in one spot. Each car that the workers built moved along the conveyor belt. As it moved, each worker added parts. This decreased wasted time. The conveyor belt also increased the number of cars produced.

On December 1, 1913, Ford introduced the moving assembly line in his factory in Highland Park, Michigan. The assembly line greatly reduced the amount of time it took to build a Model T. Before the assembly line, it took workers 12 hours to build one car. With the assembly line, it only took workers two and a half hours. These savings made the Model T much more affordable for regular people. In fact, by 1924, Ford's factory had produced 10 million Model T's.

The assembly line has improved with time and technology. Today, most factories rely on some kind of assembly line. At the Ford Motor Company's Michigan Assembly Plant, the assembly line is three miles long. About 5,000 employees work alongside 900 robots. They quickly produce a variety of vehicles. It is a far

cry from the assembly line's more humble beginnings. Still, with his basic invention and desire for efficiency, Henry Ford drove factory production into the twentieth century.

Works Cited

"Ford Installs First Moving Assembly Line: 1913." *PBS.org*, www.pbs.org/wgbh/aso/databank/entries/dt13as.html. Accessed 11 Feb. 2017.

"Ford's Assembly Line Starts Rolling." *History.com*, www.history.com/this-day-in-history/fords-assembly-line-starts-rolling. Accessed 11 Feb. 2017.

Vlasic, Bill. "100 Years Down the Line." *The New York Times*, 30 Oct. 2013, p. F1.

Dialogue: The Story Enhancer

written by Luke See

Everyone loves a great story. Whether you are reading a book or listening to a friend talk about events of the day, a good story is entertaining. What makes a story or narrative great? A strong narrative should hold a reader's attention. It should also have interesting ideas and characters. One of the best ways to enhance a narrative is to include dialogue. Dialogue helps to advance the story, develop the characters, and make the world feel real.

Dialogue enhances a narrative because it moves the plot forward. You can place important information in a conversation between characters. Imagine you are writing about two characters who are about to take a tough math test. You could just tell the reader that fact. However, it would be more interesting if you instead did it with dialogue. For example, read the following passage:

When Billy saw Samantha at lunch, he ran right up to her and said, "Are you nervous about the math exam? I feel like I haven't studied enough!"

This dialogue tells the reader about the math test in a natural way.

Dialogue helps develop a story's characters to become more interesting people. Imagine you are writing a story about a bully named Mark. You could tell the reader about some of the mean things that Mark does. However, to improve the story, you could write a scene where Mark is mean through dialogue. It will make your story more interesting. Your character will feel more realistic. Later, as Mark learns how to be a better friend, it could reflect in how he speaks through dialogue.

Finally, dialogue makes the world of your story feel more real. The more readers can place themselves in the world of a tale, the better. A fantasy story about

dragons and knights might seem unbelievable. If you include the knights arguing before a big battle, however, they will feel more like real people. If you write the words spoken by a queen as she inspires her troops, your readers will be able to visualize her and relate more closely to her. Dialogue is the perfect tool for building a realistic setting.

When you are writing a narrative story, it is easy to only focus on plot. However, by adding elements such as dialogue, you can make simple stories more exciting. Use dialogue in your narrative writing to move the action forward. If your characters seem uninteresting, give them some dialogue to make them more interesting. Dialogue is guaranteed to enhance your narrative and make your world feel more real.

Farm Living

written by Debbie Parrish
illustrated by Kevin Dinello

Have you ever wondered what it would be like to live on a family farm? Farms are located in rural or country areas where the houses are far apart. The nearest neighbor might be several miles down the road. Farm families have to drive a long way just to go to a store. That's not always a problem, though. The vegetable gardens in their backyards are loaded with tomatoes, beans, and lettuce. They taste fresher and sweeter than any that come from a can.

In the country, one will not find many major highways or streets crisscrossing the landscape. Simple two lane roads and country lanes are often all that connect different farms. There are no sidewalks on which to ride bikes, but plenty of dirt paths wind through the fields and forests.

There are many sights to see on a farm. Massive fields of corn, wheat, and grasslands surround the farm house. Barns and sheds house equipment like tractors and plows. Tall silos store harvested grains. There are pig pens, fenced areas for cows and horses, and large barns for the animals to live inside. Farm ponds supply both water for the livestock and irrigation for the hot, dry months. All around, you can hear the cows bellowing, chickens clucking, and pigs snorting. They are reminding the farmer and his family that it is feeding time.

Most farming families grow more than they can eat on their own. When a farmer plants, there is no guarantee that the crop will succeed. Sudden cold snaps can ruin vegetables. Long hot, dry weather can damage crops. Extra food never goes to waste. Farmers sell their extra crops at markets or to large companies. They sell the rest to city grocery stores.

A farming family starts its day before the sun comes up. The day does not end until long after sunset. All members of the family contribute to the farming process. Some do the hard digging and plowing. Others do tasks indoors, like keeping the books. Farmers serve as their own bookkeepers to manage money, place orders, and pay the bills.

Every season brings different chores on a farm. In early spring, farmers decide what they will plant. They also prepare the soil and plant the seeds. The growing season extends into summer. During that time, farmers must add nutrients to the soil. They also make sure the land receives enough moisture. Rain not only brings needed water—it also carries a fresh, clean smell that you just can't find anywhere else. If there is not enough water, farmers must set up large sprinklers to keep the soil moist. In summer and early fall, the family keeps busy harvesting the crops. Machines help with gathering the vegetables. Still, there is plenty to do by hand.

Raising crops is not the only work. Most farmers also keep cows, pigs, horses, and chickens. Farmers do not usually have free weekends with no work like many people who live in cities do. They must milk the cows every day of the week. They have to gather the eggs daily, as well as feed and give water to all of the animals. They clean the chicken houses, the horse stalls, and the cow barn and put down fresh straw. Only the pigs get to wallow in the mud without having their pens cleaned.

Even after the harvest season ends, farmers still keep busy. They have to can or preserve any leftover, unsold vegetables. They must plow all of the fields

before winter. Sometimes, farm equipment breaks down or becomes damaged during the harvest. Now is the time to repair or replace it.

With all of this hard work, you might ask, "What could be so great about living on a farm?" There are many reasons for farmers to like what they do. For some, it is a family tradition to work the land. A farm may have been passed down through several generations. The farmer takes pride in working the same land that his great-grandfather owned. He likes that each year, he gets to see a job done from start to finish. Farmers like the peaceful environment of the farm, the fresh breezes, the quiet, and the beautiful land.

Farm families do not usually live close to pools and parks. However, they love to enjoy a picnic on the front lawn, swim and fish in the farm pond, or hike the trails through the woods. Those same woods offer plenty of deer and other wild game to hunt for food. Instead of malls, parks, and theaters for young people, there are clubs that are geared toward farm life. One popular group is the 4-H Club. Young people join it to learn and have fun with their friends.

After sundown, when their day's work is finished, farm families like to sit on the porch together. There, they enjoy each other's company and the music of the noisy croaking frogs and buzzing insects. Even though there is much work to be done on a farm, the rewards are great. Farmers take pride in raising their own food on their own land. They enjoy caring for their animals. And when they take a moment to breathe the fresh air in their wide open space, they know the work is worth the return.

Jane Goodall

written by Summer York

When Jane Goodall was just one year old, her father gave her a stuffed ape. Her love for this toy inspired her to make great scientific discoveries.

Jane Goodall was born on April 3, 1934, in London, England. From a very early age, she was interested in nature. Her favorite childhood books included *The Jungle Book*, *Dr. Doolittle*, and *Tarzan*. These tales made her love animals. She wanted to study them in Africa. Goodall once said, "Everybody laughed at me except my amazing mother. . . [She] said, 'If you work hard and really want something and never give up, you will find a way.'"

When Goodall was in her early 20s, her dream of going to Africa came true. A friend invited Goodall to visit her in Kenya. While there, Goodall met Dr. Louis Leakey. Dr. Leakey had found many fossils in Africa. The fossils gave new information about the first humans. Leakey was impressed with Goodall's love for animals and nature. He hired her to be his assistant.

Leakey was planning to study a group of chimpanzees living in Tanzania, Africa. In July of 1960, Goodall arrived at the Gombe Stream Game Reserve in Tanzania. The Gombe Reserve was established in 1943. It protected the forests and the chimpanzees living there. Goodall planned to live on the reserve in order to study the chimpanzees in their natural habitat.

Observing the chimpanzees was not easy. At first, Goodall watched the chimps through binoculars from far away. Each time she tried to get closer, they ran from her. She needed to show the animals that she meant no harm. Every day, she went to the same spot where the chimps found food. She sat there quietly so that she would not scare them away. The chimps eventually got used to her and allowed her to come closer. After two years, the chimps learned to trust Goodall. They often allowed her to give them bananas. Goodall could now observe the chimps in a way that no one had before.

Goodall discovered many things about chimpanzees. Scientists at that time did not think that animals could have "human" qualities. Goodall, however, observed many human qualities in the chimps, including emotions and personalities. She also found out that chimps ate meat. Before this, scientists thought that chimpanzees were vegetarians, or plant-eaters.

Another one of Goodall's discoveries changed science forever. Scientists had always thought that human beings were the only species to make and use tools. However, Goodall proved that this was incorrect shortly after she arrived at the Gombe Reserve. One day, she saw a chimp stripping the leaves from a twig. He then put the twig into a log and fished out bugs to eat. This was an example of a non-human creature making and using a tool.

Goodall's findings showed that humans and chimpanzees were not as different as people had thought. In 1965, the Gombe Stream Research Center was founded. The center continued Goodall's research on chimps in the wild. Researchers there have studied Goodall's chimps for more than 50 years. Goodall's Gombe project is the longest-running research study of a species in its natural habitat.

Goodall has worked to protect chimps and other animals. In 1977, Goodall founded the Jane Goodall Institute. This organization teaches people to care for animals and the environment. She also founded Roots & Shoots, a global network of young people who serve their communities. This group works on projects that help people, animals, and the environment.

Goodall has written many books. She has traveled all over the world to talk about her research. During her travels, Goodall can often be seen holding her prized stuffed ape. It is the gift from her father. She still keeps it close after so many years. Also, no matter how far she goes, Goodall still visits Gombe National Park and her beloved chimps. Jane Goodall's adventurous, hopeful spirit inspires people everywhere to keep working for a better world.

Works Cited

"Gombe National Park." *Tanzania National Parks*, www.tanzaniaparks.go.tz/index.php?option=com_content&view=article&id=28&Itemid=186. Accessed 15 Feb. 2017.

"Gombe Stream Research Center." *The Jane Goodall Institute*, www.janegoodall.org/what-we-do/protecting-great-apes/gombe/. Accessed 15 Feb. 2017.

"Jane Goodall." *New World Encyclopedia*, 4 Aug. 2010, www.newworldencyclopedia.org/entry/Jane_Goodall. Accessed 15 Feb. 2017.

"Jane Goodall." *NNDB*. Soylent Communications, 2012. www.nndb.com/people/796/000023727/. Accessed 15 Feb. 2017.

"Jane Goodall Biography." *Biography.com*. A+E Television Networks, LLC, www.biography.com/people/jane-goodall-9542363. Accessed 15 Feb. 2017.

Jane Goodall's Roots & Shoots. The Jane Goodall Institute, www.rootsandshoots.org/. Accessed 15 Feb. 2017.

McKie, Robin. "Chimps with Everything: Jane Goodall's 50 Years in the Jungle." *The Guardian*. Guardian News and Media Limited, 27 June 2010, www.theguardian.com/science/2010/jun/27/jane-goodall-chimps-africa-interview. Accessed 15 Feb. 2017.

Moss, Stephen. "Jane Goodall: 'My Job Is to Give People Hope.'" *The Guardian*. Guardian News and Media Limited, 13 Jan. 2010, www.theguardian.com/science/2010/jan/13/jane-goodall. Accessed 15 Feb. 2017.

From Seed to Fruit

written by Luke See
illustrated by Sean Ricciardi

Many things in nature work in a cycle. For example, water moves in a cycle. It is pulled from Earth's lakes and ocean and becomes vapor in the air. That vapor forms clouds in the sky. Those clouds fill with vapor and create rain. The rain falls to the ground and returns to the lakes and oceans. From there, the water cycle begins again. Just like the water cycle, living things go through certain steps during their lifetime. Specifically, the life cycle of a plant moves in one amazing circle. A plant's life is measured by several key steps.

Where do plants come from? If you wanted to grow a sunflower or a tomato, what would you need to begin? A seed! If you plant a seed in the ground, you are beginning a plant's life cycle. Still, a seed needs a few things in order to grow. A seed should be ready to grow if it is buried in the ground somewhere where it can get water and enough sunlight. The air temperature must be right too.

Next, the seed becomes a seedling. A seedling is a small, new plant with very few leaves. A small root will emerge from the seed. The root pushes down into the ground to gather water and minerals. As the root digs downward into the earth, the stem of the new plant breaks through the soil. The stem reaches upward toward the sun. As the sun shines down on the new plant, the plant will eventually sprout leaves. The leaves then unfold, grow wider, and continue to reach for the sun.

At this stage, the plant is what is called a young adult plant. At this point, a bud will appear on the plant. A bud is a closed flower that has yet to open. Buds usually appear at the top of the stem or at the end of the leaves. As the roots continue to grow and gather minerals, the leaves keep taking in sunlight. As long as the plant remains healthy, the bud will open into a flower. A flower is not just pretty to look at. A plant that has flowered is now mature. At this stage, it is called an adult plant. The flower is extra important because it is how the plant reproduces. Reproduction allows the life cycle to continue.

Next, the flowers are pollinated. Pollination can happen in many ways. Most plants rely on pollination by way of other creatures. Bees, moths, and even bats all help pollinate plants. They do this by landing on the flower to eat nectar from the plant. They are often attracted to the bright colors of most flowers. While the insect or animal is on the flower, pollen rubs off onto the creature. When that creature lands on another flower, they carry the pollen from the first with them. This pollen fertilizes cells on the second plant. Once this happens, the plant will produce a fruit.

The fruit itself comes from the flower. The flower transforms into the fruit. This fruit is filled with seeds. The fleshy body of most fruits exists to protect the seeds as they grow and mature. As the seeds within the fruit ripen, the fruit grows larger. Once the seeds are mature, the ripened fruit will drop to the ground.

Finally, the seeds inside the fruit can begin the life cycle again. These new seeds can be spread and planted in many ways. For example, farmers and gardeners pick the fruit. People then eat and enjoy these fruits, saving the seeds. People can then plant these seeds in soil and create whole new plants. In nature, fruits may be eaten by animals that then carry the seeds inside their bodies. Once the seeds pass through the animals' stomachs and fall back to the ground, they can begin to grow into plants. Some fruits are small enough that their seeds can be carried away by the wind. These seeds are blown far and wide and will try to grow wherever they land. Seeds can also be moved by water. Rivers and streams can carry seeds for miles. Eventually, the seeds reach land and begin to grow.

Not every seed becomes a new plant. Some are destroyed. Others may end up trying to grow in soil that does not have enough nutrients, water, or sunlight. Others may be simply thrown away by people whenever they eat fruits. However, most plants produce several seeds per fruit. This gives them a better chance of restarting the life cycle once their own is complete.

Works Cited

"Fruit." *Encyclopædia Britannica*, 13 April 2018, www.britannica.com/science/fruit-plant-reproductive-body. Accessed 1 May 2018.

"Life Cycle of a Plant." *National Geographic Kids*, 4 Oct. 2017, www.natgeokids.com/za/discover/science/nature/the-life-cycle-of-flowering-plants. Accessed 2 May 2018.

"What Is Pollination?" *USDA Forest Service*, www.fs.fed.us/wildflowers/pollinators/What_is_Pollination/. Accessed 1 May 2018.

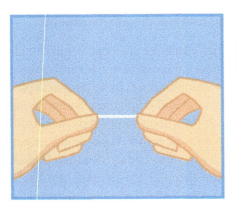 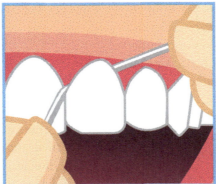 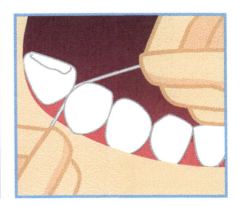

The Importance of Flossing

written by Mark Weimer

A toothbrush can only get <u>most</u> of the gunk that might be in your teeth. After you finish brushing, you should always floss between your teeth. You can get a cavity on the side of your tooth very easily. Flossing can remove gunk in between your teeth. It also prevents many other problems later in life.

If you want your teeth to be completely clean, floss after every time you brush. Flossing removes plaque from between your teeth and under your gums. Cavities can easily form in both of these places. When you remove this plaque, the fluoride in toothpaste can better cover and protect your teeth. Flossing protects your gums just as much as your teeth. Flossing strengthens your gums and prevents tartar. Tartar is plaque that has hardened. Bacteria live in tartar. Your gums can become irritated and swollen from the bacteria. This can lead to a disease called gingivitis. Other diseases can damage your jawbone. They can even cause teeth to fall out. Can you imagine your teeth just falling out of your mouth? Flossing can prevent all of this.

Your mouth is a popular location for bacteria and germs. Germs that live in an unhealthy mouth have been linked to many diseases. Poor brushing and flossing can lead to heart disease, diabetes, and many lung illnesses. Keeping your teeth clean and gums healthy is a way to protect yourself against these diseases.

Flossing also makes your visit to the dentist much better. If you do not floss, you will have a lot of tartar buildup on your teeth and in your gums. The only way to remove this is by going to the dentist. The dentist will have to <u>scrape</u> your teeth with a metal scraper. It is very uncomfortable and can sometimes make your gums bleed.

Flossing takes only a few extra minutes a day. It will remove plaque, clean out bacteria, and make trips to the dentist better. While flossing may hurt the first few times, it is well worth it. A few minutes a day can keep diseases away.

Cell Phones: Past, Present, and Future

written by Jill Fisher
illustrated by Dion Williams

Can you imagine the world without cell phones? It is not easy to picture. Today, billions of people have their very own portable phones. Believe it or not, though, only twenty years ago cell phones were extremely rare. In fact, people could only talk on the telephone by using a land line. A land line is a phone that is connected to the wall by a wire. You may have one in your home. Perhaps you have a cordless phone that is connected to your land line.

Cordless telephones are different than cell phones. A cordless phone has a base that is attached to a land line. The phone must be used within so many feet of its base or it will not work. A cell phone runs off a signal from a cell tower. Cell towers can be found all over the world. As you move, your call may switch from tower to tower without being dropped. That is how you have the freedom to talk almost anywhere while using a cell phone.

The technology used in cell phones was discovered in the late 1940s. It came along far before the invention of cell phones. The first cell phone wouldn't be introduced to the public for another forty years. These early phones had many drawbacks. They were not portable. Each was permanently attached to the inside of a car. They were often difficult to use. The line was often full of static. That made it hard to hear the person to whom you were talking. Even worse, there were many places where the phones would not work at all.

A few years later, technology advanced. People were able to remove cell phones from their cars. Sadly, they were still not very easy to use. They were large and bulky—about the size of a big briefcase. They weighed roughly twenty pounds each. They also cost a lot of money. At this time, a cell phone cost thousands of dollars. Early cell phones were meant to be used for short emergency calls. They were perfect for police cars, taxis, and military vehicles. They were not practical for the common person. Soon though, an engineer named Dr. Martin Cooper would change everything.

Dr. Martin Cooper had a vision. He believed that everyone should have a portable phone. That way, people could talk from anywhere, not just from their homes, offices, or cars. It took a lot of hard work and a team of people to reach his goal, yet he did not give up. In 1973, Dr. Cooper invented the first portable phone. It was called a handheld mobile phone. Other cell phones had existed before Dr. Cooper's invention, but they were much too bulky and heavy to be called mobile. He had a group of people create special parts that made the phone operate. Dr. Cooper also ran a contest to choose the design for the look of the phone. He picked the simplest design. The final invention was about the size of a brick.

Dr. Cooper's handheld mobile phone was a huge leap ahead. It still had some weaknesses, though. A person could only use it for a few phone calls at a time. The battery had to be charged for ten hours, but the user could only talk for thirty-five minutes. The phone only had three basic functions: dialing, listening, and talking. Still, this invention would soon help people be free to communicate from almost anywhere. By the 1990s, cell phones had become available and affordable to the average person. That is when the cell phone business began to take off.

Cell phones continue to improve as technology advances. These days, smartphone technology rivals that of the modern laptop and tablet computer. Touchscreen displays and high-quality digital cameras come standard in smartphones. Despite these new technologies and the power required to operate them, cell phones typically have excellent battery life. Most cell phones can last all day and fully charge in just a few hours, even after continuous use.

Today, cell phones can be used for much more than just sending and receiving phone calls. They are similar to mini-computers. Modern cell phones allow people to do things such as take pictures or videos, send and receive emails and text messages, listen to music, and play games. Some cell phones can give you directions when you are lost. They also allow you to check the weather and much more. They have become important tools that are used by billions all over the world.

The invention of portable cell phones has been convenient and helpful to most. However, they still need to be used with caution. There can be negative—even dangerous—side effects of using a cell phone. For example, a cell phone can be a big distraction in the car. It is very unsafe to drive a vehicle while talking on the phone. It can be even more dangerous to send and receive text messages while driving. A driver who is sidetracked by a cell phone is more likely to be in a car accident. It is important that a cell phone be put away before driving a vehicle.

In summary, cell phones allow people to talk to anyone, at anytime, from almost anywhere. This is all possible because of Dr. Martin Cooper's dream and his passion for the invention of a portable cell phone. When used safely, cell phones make staying in touch with family and friends very easy. They have become very important to people's lives. Many do not consider their cell phone a luxury, but a necessity. These once bulky, heavy machines have come a long way. They have become very useful tools that are small enough to fit right in your pocket. As technology leaps and bounds forward, cell phones will keep on changing. Expect many more advances in the future of cell phones. Just imagine what they will be able to do ten years from now!

Rain Forests: Nature's Pharmacy

written by Luke See
illustrated by Matthew Casper

Do you ever think about where medicine comes from? Although some medicines are made in a lab, most start with natural ingredients. You might be surprised to learn how many medicines come from plants that grow in rain forests. Roughly half of the world's known animal and plant species live in rain forests. It only makes sense that many medicinal plants come from rain forests. About 25 percent of all medicines come from plants. Think about how many medicines might rely on the rain forest for an ingredient! This is why it is important that rain forests are protected. Thankfully, some organizations, such as the World Wildlife Fund for Nature (WWF), are fighting to keep these lands safe.

There are many examples of rain forest ingredients used in medicines. One very important rain forest plant is the Madagascar periwinkle (*catharanthus roseus*). Also called the rosy periwinkle, the Madagascar periwinkle is a small shrub. It grows in the Madagascar rain forest. This plant has been broken down and made into some very helpful medicines. Vincristine is perhaps the most important medicine derived from the Madagascar periwinkle. Vincristine is used to treat leukemia. Thanks to this rain forest plant, 80 percent of all cases of childhood leukemia can be successfully treated. The plant is now commonly called the "Flower of Life."

The Madagascar periwinkle is just one example of a plant that has had a huge impact on medicine. The full picture of how the rain forest has helped the medical field is much larger. Rain forests must be protected. Researchers must be able to keep exploring the thousands of rain forests plants and finding new uses for them.

Madagascar periwinkle
(*catharanthus roseus*)

Works Cited

"Owed to Nature: Medicines from Tropical Forests." *Rainforest Trust,* 31 Aug. 2017, www.rainforesttrust.org/news/owed-to-nature-medicines-from-tropical-forests/. Accessed 4 May 2018.

"Why Is the Amazon Rainforest Important?" *WWF,* wwf.panda.org/what_we_do/where_we_work/amazon/about_the_amazon/why_amazon_important/. Accessed 4 May 2018.

Saving the Rain Forests

written by Luke See
illustrated by Matthew Casper

It has never been more important to protect the world's rain forests than it is today. Every day, dozens of acres of rain forest are destroyed. Large companies are ordering trees be cut down for resources. In addition, people are moving onto protected land to build houses and businesses. The rain forest is not just a beautiful place to visit and appreciate; it is also home to millions of species. Many plants and animals that can be found nowhere else call the rain forest home. Only about 7 percent of the world is covered in rain forest. However, more than 50 percent of all known animals and plants live in that small area. Rain forests truly are amazing places. For the benefit of all these animals, plants, and people, they must be protected.

Thankfully, people around the world are fighting for the rain forests. Some organizations are working to protect pieces of land in Brazil. The World Wildlife Fund for Nature (WWF) is working with the Brazilian government. The WWF is trying to put up to 10 percent of all the rain forest land under permanent government protection. Other organizations, such as the Rainforest Alliance, inspect forests to make sure they are not being damaged.

You might ask yourself, "What can I do to help the rain forests?" Raising awareness is important on its own. You can also try to shop for products that are labeled as rain forest-friendly. Looking for these labels can help you be sure your hard-earned money is supporting companies that protect the rain forests.

Works Cited

"10 Things You Can Do to Save the Rainforest." *Rainforest Foundation US*, www.rainforestfoundation.org/10-things-you-can-do-save-the-rainforest/. Accessed 4 May 2018.

"Discover Tropical Rainforests." *WWF*, wwf.panda.org/about_our_earth/deforestation/importance_forests/tropical_rainforest/. Accessed 4 May 2018.

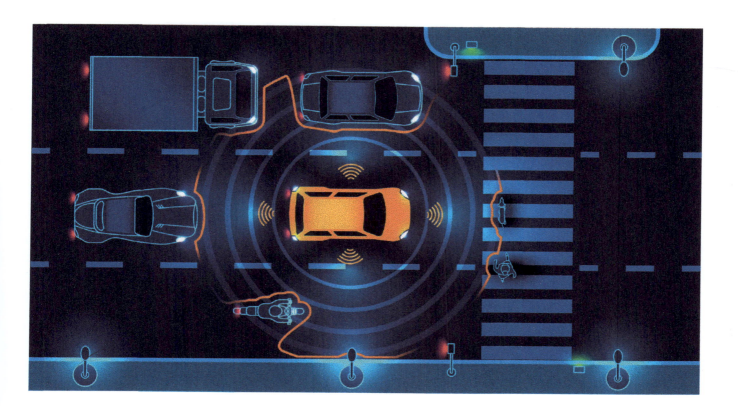

Self-Driving Cars: A Smarter Route

written by Vincent Scotto

Safety first! Four out of five car crashes in the United States occur when a human driver makes a mistake. The cost of these accidents is very high. Each day, nearly 100 people lose their lives in car accidents. However, the number of car accidents could soon significantly drop—all thanks to self-driving cars! One company has logged more than 700,000 accident-free miles already; its cars have not had any accidents to date. People who own a self-driving car are able to ride from one door to the next as a passenger. The car can also park itself without a driver behind the wheel. This will limit the time people spend parking in dangerous lots or on the street.

Self-driving cars can save lives and time. People will no longer waste time driving around in search of parking. Self-driving cars are also more fully aware of their surroundings. They can travel at higher speeds without accidents, which will cut down on travel time. Accidents will be limited to vehicle failure and road problems. These issues account for less than one-tenth of the accidents that occur today.

Self-driving cars will make life on the road safer and cheaper. They will save people time and money, but they will also save many lives. Self-driving cars might completely replace human drivers altogether one day. Everyone will be much safer and have more time. It is simply a smarter choice!

Self-Driving Cars: A Dangerous Path

written by Vincent Scotto

A self-driving car sounds pretty cool, but is it the best choice for the future? Many people do not think self-driving cars are a good idea at all. Most car accidents are caused by driver errors. Some of them are caused by vehicle malfunction. If a self-driving car has an accident, who is held responsible? No one knows. Self-driving cars also need to be able to find their passengers. People will need to share their locations to make this happen. This may become a privacy issue if people want a ride. What if they do not want to share personal information? Computers may have problems in software, too. Another person could hack into the computer that runs the car, which could be dangerous. The car might change paths suddenly! Since there is no person controlling the car, it could be used for nasty behavior.

Problems still exist with some self-driving car features. In heavy rain, the sensors have trouble reading distances from objects, which may prevent the car from stopping! Snowy roads may interfere with the cameras as well. Snow piles up high and may cause blind spots for the cameras. Self-driving cars also have trouble responding to human signals. Sometimes, the car does not move when another driver is waving it on to go.

Self-driving cars raise too many unanswered questions. One problem is not knowing whom to blame if there is an accident. Hacked car computers could be a huge problem, too. That is enough to put a halt on making too many self-driving cars. The path is still too dangerous.

How the United States Was Shaped

written by Jill Fisher
illustrated by Josh Perry

In 1776, the year of its founding, the United States of America consisted of only thirteen colonies. Today, however, America is composed of fifty states. Forty-eight of these states are located between two countries and three large bodies of waters. These states are known as the continental, or mainland, United States. The nation of Canada borders the mainland to the north, while Mexico meets its southern border. The bordering bodies of water are the Pacific Ocean on the west, the Atlantic Ocean on the east, and the Gulf of Mexico along parts of the south. The remaining two states are separate from the mainland. The forty-ninth state, Alaska, is divided from the mainland by Canada. Alaska is located about five hundred miles northwest of the state of Washington. The fiftieth state, Hawaii, is even farther away. Made up of a group of islands in the Pacific Ocean, Hawaii is over two thousand miles southwest of California.

Each of the fifty states has a unique shape and size. Many factors affected the crazy borders of the jigsaw puzzle that make up the United States. Some borders were created by natural elements, such as rivers, lakes, volcanoes, and mountain ranges. However, military battles, historical events, railroads, the government, and more played a hand as well.

Mother Nature helped to create some of the more oddly-shaped states with her enormous mountain ranges, dangerous volcanoes, great lakes, and powerful rivers. Twelve states have borders that are marked by active or potentially active volcanoes. They are Alaska, Arizona, California, Colorado, Hawaii, Idaho, New

Mexico, Nevada, Oregon, Utah, Washington, and Wyoming. Many other states are divided by rivers. For example, the southern part of Ohio is lined by the Ohio River. This river marks the border between Ohio and the states of West Virginia and Kentucky.

Over time, some rivers have shifted due to erosion. That makes some parts of states appear to be on the wrong side of the rivers that originally marked their borders. For example, part of Indiana's border was originally marked by the Wabash River. Today, though, there are small parts of Indiana that are on the wrong side of this river. They look like they are part of Illinois due to the Wabash River gradually shifting over a long period of time. Obviously, this can be quite confusing.

Another reason for confusing borders between the states is human error. Long ago, when the states were created, men surveyed the land using transit and compass, chronometer, and astronomical readings. They also relied on information from previous surveys. They did the best they could with the given tools and situation. The border between the states of Georgia and Tennessee is still debated today. People say the original border is incorrect and needs to be changed. It is believed that the surveyor started at the wrong location. In fact, there are some homes that use Georgia addresses, even though they are technically in the state of Tennessee.

State boundaries have also been formed by historical events, such as the Louisiana Purchase, the creation of the Mason-Dixon Line, and the Oregon Treaty. The Mason-Dixon Line, for instance, takes its name from two surveyors named Charles Mason and Jeremiah Dixon. They helped to settle a dispute in colonial times over where Pennsylvania ended and where the colonies

to the south of it began. The line these men mapped forms the southern border of Pennsylvania and the western border of Delaware. It sets these states off from Maryland and West Virginia (which was still part of Virginia when the line was drawn).

Look carefully at a map of America. You will notice how the states on the eastern side of the country have crooked borders and widely varying sizes. The states farther west look more like organized squares with straight lines. That is because people occupied the eastern side early in the country's history, with each state making its own rules. However, as the United States expanded westward, the American government made laws about how to form the states. In fact, most borders beyond the original thirteen colonies were created by Congress, which gave the states a more uniform shape and size. Often, they used the lines of longitude and latitude to determine the size and shape of each state.

Some states are very large while others are tiny. As the states were being formed, many people believed that all states should be the same size. In fact, back in 1786, Thomas Jefferson predicted the large territory of California would crumble into smaller states. Despite border battles, the gold rush, and even earthquakes, that did not happen. Another large state, Texas, was created with the intention of dividing it into five smaller states. Obviously, that did not happen either.

It is clear that many forces have affected the size and shape of each of the states. Over time, Mother Nature will continue to change the earth, and there may be more historical events that change the shapes of the states. Will the map of the United States ever look different than it does now? Only time will tell.

The Pacific Coast Gem: A Memorable Tour by Train

*A Coastal Railways Travel Guide, written by Sarah Marino
illustrated by Mallory Senich*

The California coast is perhaps one of the most wondrous sights to behold. From rugged mountains to pristine beaches, this stretch of the United States is a feast for the senses. Let Coastal Railways introduce you to this magical place and give you one of your best vacations yet. Make the Pacific Coast Gem train ride your next adventure!

To start, you will tour through the North Coast Redwoods. These are some of the biggest trees in the world! Glorious canopies of green surround you as you view the forest from every angle. Stopping in the small town of Eureka, you can smell fragrant air, some of the purest in the country. Whiffs of pine and salty ocean water will surely leave you refreshed and ready for the next part of the journey.

San Francisco is a city unlike any other. It is beautiful and rugged all at once. As it is the next stop on the Pacific Coast Gem tour, you will have time to explore. The Golden Gate Bridge is a marvel of engineering, and the mountains it is nestled between are likewise awe-inspiring. Whether under a clear, sunny sky or in the midst of the city's famed fog, this vista is one you will never forget. The deep red color of the bridge both contrasts and blends into the surrounding landscape. Be sure to walk across it to explore the bridge and see the view from this special place.

As you enter the city near Fisherman's Wharf, you may hear a strange barking sound. Don't be alarmed! That is simply the lovely sound of the sea lions who reside near Pier 39 at the wharf. These cute creatures add charm to an already picturesque tourist attraction.

Continue your tour by heading farther into the city. Hopefully you brought walking shoes because the hills of San Francisco are intense! They can be quite the workout. Beautiful homes of many different pastels and styles line the streets and please the eye. As you walk, don't forget to check out Lombard Street, whose first block consists of eight tight zig-zag turns. Remember, too, that San Francisco is on the Pacific Coast! Wander around Ocean Beach and dip your toes in the chilly water. Then head back through Golden Gate Park; inhale the scent of the cypress trees and the gorgeous roses at the Conservatory of Flowers.

Heading south and a bit inland, the Pacific Coast Gem train ride steams into Santa Clara Valley. There lies Silicon Valley, the technology headquarters of the United States. Nestled between the Santa Cruz Mountains and the Diablo Range is the city that is considered the heart of Silicon Valley, San Jose. The inland climate is much different from that of San Francisco. Temperatures can reach into the triple-digits in the summer months. The surrounding mountain hills are covered with dry grasses and desert vegetation. Mount Hamilton, the highest peak in San Jose, is home to Lick Observatory, an astronomy laboratory run by the University of California. The city of San Jose itself is quite flat, with none of the steep city hills for which San Francisco is famous. After briefly touring some of the major businesses in the area, you will get a chance to see Moffett Airfield, a NASA research center, as well as Stanford University.

Heading back out to the coast and along Highway 1, the Gem makes its way into some of the most pristine, gorgeous coastline of the United States, named Big Sur. Sharp, rocky cliffs jut out of the ocean, which sparkles a lovely aquamarine. Lush green vegetation and evergreens sit atop the rugged cliffs. These vistas will surely take your breath away!

The next stop is home to some of the most famous sea life in the world. Welcome to Monterey and the well-known Monterey Bay Aquarium. This city on the Pacific boasts beautiful seascapes and small-town charm. If you brought your wetsuit, be sure to check out the surfing scene!

The nearby town of Carmel is also a sightseeing favorite, with white-sand beaches and quaint tiny streets like those in European villages. The town is also home to one of the oldest Roman Catholic Mission churches in the United States, founded in the late 1700s. The cypress trees are extraordinary—especially to those who hail from the East Coast!

The coast past Carmel marks the southern edge of Big Sur. Its rolling green hills and rocky cliffs and beaches, with mountains off to the east, make for a delightful ride into Southern California. Soon you will enter the City of Angels! Los Angeles, in the San Fernando Valley, is a city of sprawl. However, it is beautiful nonetheless. Tour the beaches of Venice, Malibu, and Santa Monica, and make sure to check out the Hollywood spectacle. Continue south to San Diego to see world-famous beaches and more rugged, mountainous canyons. This last stop on the Gem train ride provides a fairytale ending to a fantastic exploration of the Pacific Coast. Book your seats today!

The Koala

written by Luke See
illustrated by Walter Sattazahn

Background

What do you know about the koala? Maybe you have heard this furry little creature called a "koala bear." This is a common misconception, or wrong idea. The koala is actually a marsupial. Marsupials are mammals that carry their young in a pouch on their body. This means that the koala is more closely related to the kangaroo than to any bear. Like kangaroos, baby koalas are also called joeys. After it is born, a koala baby can be carried in its mother's pouch for up to seven months! Koalas are easy to recognize. They range in color from silver to brown. They have large round faces and big fluffy ears. They also have unique noses that give them a cute look. The koala is a fascinating creature that needs a specific diet and habitat in order to live and thrive.

Habitat

Koalas are found only on the Australian continent. Specifically, most koalas live on the eastern part of the country. They live in such a precise area because of the habitat on which they depend. Koalas live in eucalyptus trees, high off the ground. The eucalyptus tree is not just a comfy spot for koalas to live—they are important to the animal's survival. These trees provide koalas with all the food they need. The big appetite of an individual koala can actually be a threat to their habitat. If an area has too many koalas, they can destroy entire trees! They do this by eating all the leaves before the tree can grow more. Their own big appetites are not the only threat to their habitat, however. About 80 percent of the koala's original habitat is now gone. This is partly because of people moving farther into forests and tearing down eucalyptus trees. Natural issues such as droughts and forest fires have also limited the number of eucalyptus trees.

Diet

A koala's entire diet consists of leaves from the eucalyptus tree. These leaves are also known as gum leaves. Gum leaves are very fibrous and hard to eat. They are also very low in nutrition. Because of this, eucalyptus leaves take a lot of energy to digest. Koalas rest or sleep about 22 hours every day! They rest this long due to the amount of energy their body needs to digest their food. By sleeping, koalas save energy and can fully digest the eucalyptus leaves. The gum leaves do have a few benefits, however. First, they are poisonous to many other animals. This is good for koalas because all the leaves are left for them. Koalas have a special organ called a cecum that breaks the eucalyptus leaves down. The leaves also carry a lot of water. Because of this, koalas rarely have to drink anything. In fact, the native people of Australia—the Aborigines—gave the koala its name. In the Aboriginal language, the word *koala* means "no drink."

Works Cited

"10 Facts about Koalas!" *National Geographic Kids*, 1 Feb. 2017, www.natgeokids.com/uk/discover/animals/general-animals/ten-facts-about-koalas. Accessed 3 May 2018.

"Koala." *Encyclopædia Britannica*, 27 April 2018, www.britannica.com/animal/koala. Accessed 3 May 2018.

"Physical Characteristics of the Koala." *Australian Koala Foundation*, www.savethekoala.com/about-koalas/diet-habitat. Accessed 2 May 2018.

Benefits of Children Learning a Musical Instrument

written by Katie Catanzarite

What thing do movies, TV shows, and musicals almost always have in common? That common thing is music. Music can be subtle. Sometimes, TV shows need a small melody to pair with a dramatic scene. Music can also be grand. A musical often features one big song right before the intermission. Including music in entertainment offers many benefits. There are even more advantages when you can play an instrument yourself. When young children learn how to play a musical instrument, it can improve their work ethic, teach them how to pay attention to detail, and open different doors of opportunity.

Learning how to play a musical instrument can improve your work ethic. Many musicians begin their careers at a young age. A majority of instruments, such as the piano and guitar, involve using both hands. They call for the musician to be able to read notes. Think of your favorite singer. He or she probably knows how to read music on some level. How long does it take a person to learn an instrument well enough to play in front of an audience? The work usually must begin early. At the age of eight, a child may learn scales and chords. By the age of eighteen, the child may have grown into an adult who is able to play Beethoven. You gain an understanding of your chosen instrument, but you also learn discipline and the value of practice. You can apply these strategies to schoolwork or sports. Learning a musical instrument teaches you that hard work will pay off.

Learning a musical instrument also teaches you how to pay attention to detail. When learning any instrument, musicians must keep many tiny details in mind. Musicians must learn how to position their fingers. They must learn how to make different kinds of sounds. They must learn how to control their volume. If

you can learn all the details of an instrument, then you can understand how to view a problem from multiple angles. You will know how to tweak something just enough to make an overall improvement.

Learning a musical instrument offers many new opportunities. Not all musicians go on to play in the symphony. However, they may earn a living by writing music—maybe for one of those TV shows or movies they love. They may also be special librarians who recommend music instead of books. They may even become music therapists. Music therapists help the ill through music. If you learn how to play an instrument early on, you may have an advantage in the future.

Of course, not everyone will go on to be the next Mozart. Even so, musical instruments teach skills that are hard to gain otherwise. Learning a musical instrument at a young age improves your work ethic. It also teaches you how to pay attention to detail. Finally, it opens different doors of opportunity. Playing an instrument is not easy, but there is nothing sweeter than seeing all of your practice pay off.

George the Great and Powerful

written by Jennifer Tkocs

I didn't always want to be a magician. In fact, I spent most of my early years hoping to be president of a successful company, like my dad. But everything changed one day when I was nine years old.

Each autumn, the circus came to our town. It stayed for two weeks, and each year, my siblings and I tried to see as many of the exhibits as we could. My twelve-year-old sister, Lindsay, loved the elephants. She hoped someday to be a veterinarian. My eldest brother, Michael, loved the daredevil acts. He was trying to restore a rusty old motorcycle in our garage, now that he was old enough to ride one.

My favorite part of the circus was the magic show. Each time the circus visited, the famous magician, Anthony Marvel, held daily magic shows in his own tent. As soon as school ended each day, I rushed to the fairgrounds to watch.

Although I loved Anthony Marvel's shows, I never dreamed that I, too, could be a magician. His tricks were phenomenal. I asked Michael once how he thought Anthony Marvel made doves appear out of thin air.

"Some people are just born with magic in their blood," Michael told me.

I wished that I had been born that way. I'd been born so ordinary. I was as ordinary as a stale box of crackers. I could barely get bread to toast without burning it. There was no way I could ever do the awesome tricks that Anthony Marvel did.

Year after year, I sat in the front row of Anthony Marvel's shows, watching. I watched him saw his assistant in half dozens of times. Each time, she emerged in one piece. She never even flinched when the saw cut through her like a knife cutting through

butter. I didn't know how it worked every time. It was just magic, I guessed. That's all there was to it.

One day, I met up with Lindsay after the magic show. "George, guess what?" she said. "I met the elephant trainer. She noticed me spending so much time around their pen every day. And guess what else?"

"She thinks you look like an elephant and would fit right in with them?" I said.

Lindsay crossed her arms. "Not at all! You're so rude! She said that I could help her give the elephants baths. And she will teach me more about them. I'll be a master elephant trainer in no time!"

I scowled. That wasn't fair. How did Lindsay get to make friends with her idol? I was just a perpetual audience member. Anthony Marvel didn't even know I existed. *He must know I don't have any magic in my blood*, I thought.

The next day, I thought about skipping the magic show. I felt as low as a beetle after learning that Lindsay was going to be the elephant trainer's apprentice.

Michael was probably going to finish his motorcycle before winter. They were both going to run off to join the circus, and I was still going to be the same old George, boring as plain oatmeal, stuck at home.

But something at the last minute convinced me to go. What if Anthony Marvel debuted a fantastic new trick and I missed it? Even worse, what if Lindsay went and I didn't, and then Anthony Marvel asked her to be his new assistant? I couldn't risk it.

Even though I was feeling bad, I dragged myself to the magic show. I got my usual spot in the front row and settled in. What magic would Anthony Marvel show us today?

He breezed through a few of his regular tricks; flowers jumped out of nowhere, and rabbits seemed to replicate before our very eyes. Then, he called out into the crowd for a volunteer. My hand shot up into the air. "Ah, yes, the young gentleman in the front row," Anthony Marvel said.

I couldn't believe he picked me! Out of all the times I'd volunteered at one of his shows, he had never chosen me to go on stage. My feet were cement blocks as I made my way up the wooden steps. My heart was a prisoner trying to leap out of its cage.

"Now I am going to do a card trick," he said. "This is a very complicated trick, and it requires you to focus. Can you promise you will focus as hard as you can?"

"I'm a laser beam," I assured Anthony Marvel. "I'm perfectly focused!"

"Excellent. I am going to hold out these cards, and I'll need you to choose one." He fanned the cards out in front of me, and I picked one from the middle. "Remember what your card is," he told me. "You can hold the card out to the audience and show them. I will look away."

I looked down at the card in my hand. It was the ace of spades. I did my best to conceal it from Anthony Marvel. Carefully, I turned to face the audience and showed them my card, keeping it hidden from the magician behind me.

As I held the card up, though, I noticed something on the back. There, woven into the design on the card, was a little notch. It was barely noticeable, but the light caught it in just a way that I could see it. I wondered what it meant. Maybe it was just a misprint.

"All right, son, please place your card back into this deck," Anthony Marvel said. I slid the card into a different space in the deck. As I did, the cards on either side slid apart from each other, and I noticed that they, too, had notches in the back. They were in different locations than the notch on my card.

"I will shuffle this deck three times," Anthony Marvel said. "I will then place the deck beneath my trusty rabbit. A magical rabbit like that only increases the magic in the deck of cards."

I watched as Anthony Marvel did his showmanship bit. The cards danced between his hands, but I was only half-paying attention. *What was the meaning of those notches on the cards?* I wondered. I barely heard as Anthony Marvel plucked my card out from under the rabbit. "Mister Nibbles was sitting on top of an ace of spades. Was that your card?"

"It was," I said. "Thank you."

The crowd burst into applause, but I was a hundred miles away, lost in thought. *It wasn't magic at all*, I realized. The different notches in the card design—they had to mean something. I had to get ahold of that deck.

Later that evening, after the magic show ended, I went to visit Lindsay at the elephant pen. "I need your help," I told her. I knew she would stay late after the other circus staff had gone home. "Let me stay here with you when you put the elephants to bed."

Lindsay was suspicious, but she agreed. "If you get me into trouble," she warned, "you're dead meat!"

"I won't," I promised.

I waited around with her, watching the other circus members leave for the day. At last, Anthony Marvel walked out. He was not carrying anything with him. Perfect; this meant he had left his deck of cards.

I slipped quietly into the magic tent. There was no one around to notice me, but I crept as quietly as one of Anthony Marvel's rabbits, just in case. Backstage, tables were set up with the magician's props. There, at the end of the table, was the deck of cards. Checking one last time to make sure no one was around, I snatched it up and put it in my pocket.

That night at home, I studied the cards. It only took a few minutes to unlock the secret the playing cards were keeping. Spades had markings in the bottom left corner, clubs had markings in the top left corner, and hearts and diamonds had markings on the right side. The marks were placed inside a circle, like hands on a clock with thirteen numbers.

That's it, I thought. *He can see the back of the card. He can read the placement of the notch, and that's how he can tell which card you've pulled, even without seeing the front!*

I realized that there was no magic involved. It was just skill and careful attention to detail. What if every trick was like this? What if all magic was just sleight of hand or a quickly performed illusion?

As I sat in my room that night with Anthony Marvel's trick deck of cards, I realized that my brother had been wrong. You weren't born with magic in your blood. You were born with the desire to entertain. You had to learn the magic to reach this goal. My life was never going to be the same.

Betrayal of Mathematical Proportions

written by Summer York

The cafeteria buzzed with activity as students filed in and greeted friends.

"Hey!" Cam announced to the table, sliding into a chair and slinging his bookbag on the floor. "Paul, where were you this morning? You weren't in homeroom. Didn't think you'd show today."

"I missed the bus," Paul replied through a yawn, "so my mom had to drive me."

"Oh, trying to get out of the big math test today, huh?" Cam joked between mouthfuls of peanut butter and jelly.

"Yeah, right," Paul said defensively. "I was up really late studying, and I slept through my alarm." *Not that all of that studying helped at all*, Paul thought anxiously. Today, Mr. Rider's third grade math classes were taking an exam on division with decimal numbers. It seemed to Paul that he was having more of a tough time understanding the concept than the other students. The decimal point always ended up in the wrong place. Long division was hard enough—why did they have to throw in decimal points too?

Cam sensed his friend's misery. "It won't be that bad," he told Paul.

"I'm gonna fail, I just know it," Paul vented. "I'll fail math, have to repeat third grade, and be kicked out of school because I can't do long division!" Paul groaned and leaned his forehead on the table. Cam rolled his eyes at his friend's dramatic rant. Suddenly, Paul whipped his head up, and his eyes opened wide.

"Wait, you're good at math—I can copy your answers!" Paul gushed. "We sit next to each other, so it's perfect. Just slide your test toward the edge of your desk so I can see it."

"Um, I don't know..." Cam hesitated. Just then, the bell rang to signal the end of lunch. It was time for math class.

"You have to," Paul urged. "It's the only way I'll pass."

Cam was quiet as they left the cafeteria.

In class, Mr. Rider passed out the exams and told the students to start. Paul kept waiting for Cam to show his paper, but he never did. He would not even look in Paul's direction. Paul felt a swell of terror and fury rising in his throat. His mind went as blank as the paper in front of him. A cold sweat clammed up on his shaking hands, and his brain could form only one thought: He had been betrayed.

At the sound of the bell, all of the students turned in their exams and headed out the door. Cam rushed to get out quickly, but Paul was right behind him.

"Cam!" Paul yelled angrily, grabbing Cam's bookbag to stop him from getting away. "I thought you were gonna let me copy your answers. How could you betray me like that?"

"How could you ask me to help you cheat?" Cam demanded.

Paul balled his fists tightly at his sides, trying to control his rage. "I just failed that test because of you!" His tears were hot streams on his cheeks, and he frantically wiped them away. "We're not friends anymore!" Paul announced, storming off down the hallway.

Sunrise in the Desert

written by Jennifer Tkocs
illustrated by Brittanie Markham

The sun rises
Shadows shift across the rocks
Lizards poke up their heads
And come out from rocky nests
They feel the sun warm their scales

Across the sand
The bighorn sheep awaken
They nibble breakfast grasses
And sniff the dry air
They smell the scent of desert flowers

Eight furry legs
Skitter across rough pebbles
The hungry tarantula begins
Its morning hunt for bugs
The most fun part of its day

Slowly
Nervously
With careful steps
The tortoise creeps across the road
Looking for a safe, sunny spot

A cool breeze
Blows the leaves of the Joshua tree
The leaves flutter loudly
Morning has arrived
Across the desert

A Girl's Future

written by Summer York

A girl's future is a vast expanse of hope and
possibilities. It spreads out before her like
an infinite ocean. A girl's potential is
limited only by her dreams. She could be anything,
from a famous athlete, to a factory worker.
Maybe she wants to be a doctor, healing the sick,
or a lawyer who fights against injustice. Maybe she'll be
a teacher, molding and inspiring young minds, or she'll be
a valiant soldier who risks all to protect her country's freedom.
She could be a farmer, pouring her sweat into America's heartland.
She could be a brilliant scientist who makes new discoveries.
She might be a police officer or a firefighter or an emergency
responder—someone who runs toward danger to save lives.
She might desire a career in politics, hoping to create new
and better laws, like George Washington and Abraham Lincoln.
Her goals might not be quite so far-reaching.
She could work in construction, building America's forest-like skyline.
She might like to serve food at a restaurant or count money at a bank.
She does not need a well-known name or lots of money; she has changed
the world just by chasing her dreams.

Strength

written by Summer York

I must be strong like a mighty mountain—steady, immovable—

in times of turmoil. I shall not yield to

wind or rain or the strongest of nature's fury.

But one rumble of the earth can bring a mountain crashing

down. A mountain is too rigid—not flexible.

No, I will not be a mountain.

Instead, I will be strong like a regal oak tree, rooted

solidly in the ground yet swaying with the winds.

As fierce storms rage, the great oak bends so it does

not break. Its heavy roots hold fast, planted firmly to

stand in the face of turbulence.

Rain and Baseball

written by Steve Karscig

Rain and baseball just do not mix.
Those heavy drops and dark clouds
dampen my ability to catch.
When the sand turns to sludge
and the outfield becomes a marsh,
I can feel the mucky misery of moisture
in every soaked step and every touch.
A slick bat and soaked mitt
drips nine innings from my grip.
I await the sun and fateful phrase
when hoping to "play ball" again.

Climbing Magnolias

written by Steve Karscig

Blooming in pink and white,
the magnolia pushes out the winter night.
Its smooth gray bark, hard as stone,
does not detract from the beauty it shows.

When flowers fade and leaves take their place,
children will decorate the magnolia in haste.
The magnolia holds laughter in place of its flowers,
as boys and girls climb on the strong branches at all hours.

Like a smile for sunshine, the art of climbing surely fades
when the storms of the season and adulthood take it away.
Ready for another winter, the magnolia becomes bare,
but does the tree remember who was there?

Swinging on Weeping Willows

written by Steve Karscig
illustrated by Brittanie Markham

When I picture my favorite tree,
a willow for me, it will certainly be.
Weeping branches barely touching ground,
I reach to grab them and swing around.

Other poets prefer birches and oaks,
and I will admit that I admire such folks.
Yet, it is just the willow for me;
it is simply a great swinging tree.

There's certainly something about the willow
that I wish to share with every fellow.
It hides this secret in its bladed leaves:
Sometimes a weeping tree provides the best company.

The Great Aluminum Knight

written by Steve Karscig
illustrated by Dave Rushbrook

Cast

DOUGRAY THE BRAVE .... A boy looking for adventure through fantasy playtime

MARTIN THE TORMENTOR .... A child with a mean streak

JOSIE THE KEEN .... A smart girl

SYLVESTER THE SINISTER .... Martin's friend; a follower

PHOEBE THE FEEBLE .... A shy girl

HAWK .... An ordinary predatory bird from the raptor family

Setting

A neighborhood playground with a swing set, merry-go-round, surrounding trees, and other playful structures.

– 161 –

<u>Scene One</u>

Scene: *A lively public playground filled with children, parents, and well-kept playground equipment. A four-person swing set stands at center stage, with a large tree in the background.*

Four children are swinging on the swing set: MARTIN, SYLVESTER, JOSIE, and PHOEBE. Enter DOUGRAY. He walks to the side of the swing set and slides off his backpack. He kneels down and opens the backpack. He pulls out a box of aluminum foil and a piece of old broken fence lattice.

MARTIN [*swinging on swing*]: Dou-gray…Douggie…Dooger…Hey, Dummy! [*laughing forcibly*] What are you doing in my playground?

DOUGRAY [*looking over from one knee*]: I am preparing to play something epic, if you must know.

SYLVESTER [*taunting*]: Oh, did you hear that? Somethin' epic.

DOUGRAY [*still kneeling*]: Do you even know what "epic" means?

MARTIN: 'Course we do. Whaddaya think we are, some kinda molasses-brained morons?

JOSIE [*swinging on swing*]: Ugh…. "Epic" means something that is part poetry-like and part adventure-like. Princesses and castles, heroic deeds and lost loves, swords and sorcery—a chosen warrior against the world they live in. It's something fantastical.

DOUGRAY: Yeah, roughly like that.

JOSIE: Dougie, I don't understand why you would do something like that in front of these two fools. You know they are just going to make fun of you.

DOUGRAY: Even a hero of experience must tolerate fools.

DOUGRAY begins wrapping the piece of old lattice with some aluminum foil.

MARTIN: What experience do you have? We're all in the same class. There is nothing special about you. You're a daydreamer. That's why Miss Thompson makes fun of you.

PHOEBE [*chewing on her hair, speaking meekly*]: Miss Thompson makes fun of everybody. She's not very nice.

SYLVESTER [*to DOUGRAY*]: What are you makin', anyway?

DOUGRAY: I am creating my own sword like Arthur's Excalibur, Roland's Durandal, and Beowulf's Naegling.

MARTIN: W-what?

JOSIE: They're famous sword names from legends. Don't you know that?

DOUGRAY holds up his wooden sword made from the broken lattice, which is now covered in aluminum foil. The light shines on it, allowing the foil to sparkle. The children on the swings giggle.

DOUGRAY: Behold! I give you the sword, the greatest of all warrior weaponry!

MARTIN: Man, I've thrown away better toys than that!

Enter the HAWK, a wild animal not particularly concerned with the children. The HAWK circles and then perches on a low-hanging tree branch in the playground.

SYLVESTER [*jumping off the swing*]: Whoa, would ya look at that! It's an eagle.

JOSIE: It's a hawk. Eagles are bigger. Sheesh.

MARTIN [*leaping from his swing*]: I'll bet I can knock it down with a rock.

SYLVESTER: Do it!

JOSIE: No! Leave it alone. It's a keystone species. It is important to the environment.

MARTIN: Shut it! I got this.

MARTIN picks up three small rocks from the ground. In the same moment, though, the HAWK flies off.

SYLVESTER: Aw, man!

MARTIN watches off-stage closely.

MARTIN: No, it's all right. He just went to that other tree by the merry-go-round. Let's go, nice and quiet.

PHOEBE: Please don't hurt the bird.

Scene Two

Scene: *MARTIN and SYLVESTER have moved around the tree to the area of the park where the merry-go-round is posted. All of the other children, except for DOUGRAY, have followed him. JOSIE and PHOEBE sit on the still merry-go-round. The HAWK curiously watches the children's movements.*

MARTIN: I need to get a clear shot. I don't want to miss this.

DOUGRAY enters. He is now dressed in epic aluminum armor, with sword in hand, looking like a knight. He steps up behind MARTIN and reaches his free hand out.

DOUGRAY: Stop!

MARTIN: What?

MARTIN turns to face DOUGRAY and laughs hysterically.

SYLVESTER [*pushing DOUGRAY*]: Shut up, Doogie.

DOUGRAY: Insolent peasant!

DOUGRAY swings at SYLVESTER with his makeshift sword and whacks him in the arm.

– 163 –

SYLVESTER: Ouch!

> *MARTIN turns from the HAWK and throws one of his three rocks at DOUGRAY. It dents his aluminum foil breastplate and makes him stumble backward.*

MARTIN: Not so tough now, are you?

> *DOUGRAY swings his sword at MARTIN but misses.*

DOUGRAY: Umph!

> *MARTIN throws his remaining two rocks at DOUGRAY, hitting him again in the chest.*

MARTIN: Take that!

> *DOUGRAY holds his chest painfully. He looks up at the HAWK.*

DOUGRAY: Fly! Fly, bird. Fly away!

> *DOUGRAY tosses his sword up toward the tree, hitting the branch upon which the HAWK is perched. The HAWK takes flight and soars well out of harm's reach, away from the children. DOUGRAY'S shining sword is stuck in the tree branches.*

> *MARTIN pushes DOUGRAY, ripping the aluminum armor from his chest.*

MARTIN: Was that epic enough for you, loser? You lost your fake sword and your pretend armor, and now you have nothing to play with. Not even friends.

> *MARTIN and SYLVESTER exit. JOSIE stands up on the merry-go-round.*

JOSIE: Hooray, Dougray the Brave, Defender of the Hawk! That was truly epic.

DOUGRAY: It felt epic. [*coughing and rubbing his chest*] Not particularly what I had in mind, though. I lost my sword.

PHOEBE [*chewing on her hair*]: Trees have been known to take all types of toys from kids.

JOSIE: You didn't lose it! You made a sacrifice play for the good of the hawk. You saved an animal from a cruel fate. Like the sword in the stone, your sword is now a majestic symbol. [*pointing to the sword hanging by the branches*] Talon should be its name!

DOUGRAY: Yeah, sure.

> *DOUGRAY pulls off the last bits of his aluminum armor and walks away, discouraged. PHOEBE pulls her hair out of her mouth.*

PHOEBE: Our hero!

END OF PLAY

The Vision of Gwen

written by Steve Karscig

<u>Cast</u>

MOTHER... GWEN'S mom; early 30s
GWEN .... daughter; nine years old

<u>Setting</u>

The kitchen of a Craftsman-style home.

Scene: *An ordinary kitchen in a Craftsman-style home. Cabinets, a countertop, and a window are in the background. MOTHER cooks stew on the stove. A kitchen table with four chairs stands in the foreground.*

Enter GWEN, a child of nine years. She wears a pink shirt, khaki slacks, purple glasses, and blue canvas tennis-style shoes.

GWEN [*shutting the door*]: Hi, Mom. I'm home.

MOTHER [*stirring the pot of stew*]: Hi, sweetie. How was your day?

GWEN sits at the kitchen table.

GWEN: What are you doing?

MOTHER: I'm making stew for dinner. You didn't answer me.

GWEN: Oh, my day was fine.

MOTHER: Just fine? [*smelling the stew*] I think I might have over-done it on the onion powder.

GWEN: Well, there is this little thing I have been thinking about.

MOTHER turns and looks at GWEN.

MOTHER: And…?

GWEN: Do you remember when you said I could get contact lenses when I turn 10?

MOTHER: I do. When you are ten, you can get them.

GWEN: Well, I was wondering….

MOTHER [*interrupting*]: When you are 10.

GWEN: Just hear me out on this one.

MOTHER: We've already had this discussion plenty of times.

MOTHER returns to stirring the stew.

GWEN: I am nine years old now. Ten is a full year away. But if you let me get them now, I thought I could….

MOTHER [*turning to face GWEN*]: Honey, contacts aren't all they're cracked up to be. You could go blind using them if you don't care for them correctly. Besides, I think you look fabulous in your glasses.

GWEN takes off her glasses and sets them on the table.

GWEN: Mom, I look like a little girl in these. Joey Harvey said that I look the same as I did in the third grade. I am ready to take some new steps and experience some new things in my life.

MOTHER [*pointing the stirring spoon at GWEN*]: Really? If you want to experience some new things, the recycling under the sink can go out to the tub.

GWEN: Mom! This is important! I want to see without glasses for once in my life.

MOTHER [*chuckling*]: All right. Continue.

GWEN: The fourth-grade dance is coming up, and I thought I would look just fabulous in my dress from Easter, but without my purple glasses. I want to show off my best feature.

>   *GWEN quickly blinks her eyes repeatedly.*

MOTHER [*stirring the stew again*]: Your dress is pink. Pink and purple go together just fine.

>   *GWEN gets up from the table and reaches under the sink to retrieve the recycling.*

GWEN: Ugh, I know, but I want to be more refined—you know, classy and beautiful. Like a princess.

MOTHER [*watching GWEN gather the recycling*]: Sweetie, you are classy and beautiful, and you will always be my princess. I have a feeling this is not entirely about contact lenses.

GWEN [*looking embarrassed*]: Yes, it is, Mom. What else would it be about? Humph.

MOTHER: You take out the recycling, and I will have an answer for you when you come back inside.

>   *Exit GWEN. Plastic bottles and cans bang around inside a container offstage.*

MOTHER [*looking up at the ceiling*]: Oh, I am so not ready for this.

>   *GWEN re-enters, wearing a cheesy, exaggerated smile.*

GWEN: So?

MOTHER [*sighing*]: We will go on Saturday so you can try them. You might not like contacts.

GWEN: Yay! I will. I will love them.

MOTHER: But you will have some extra chores to do around here, princess!

END OF SCENE

Stone Soup

a play in one act
adapted by Michael Scotto
illustrated by Dion Williams

Cast

PÉTER (PAY-tur)	age 21, clever, thoughtful
PATRIK	age 24, haughty, impatient
IVAN	age 53, a towering, bullying butcher
MARIA	age 38, suspicious
DAVOS	age 42, bearded bake shop owner
MINYA	age 68, kindly villager
ANDRAS	age 29, another villager

Setting

An afternoon in August, 1789. Locations include a country road in the nation of Hungary, and the town square of the village of Folàsz, Hungary.

SCENE ONE

Scene: *A dirt country road in central Hungary. Rocks are scattered about the road, and a river runs along behind it. PATRIK, a rail-thin twenty-four-year-old, sleeps near the river on the side of the road. He is using a large stone for a pillow. His clothes are dirty and faded, except for spots that have been patched over. The patches on his clothes are colorful, bright material. PATRIK coughs, then settles down, snoring gently.*

PATRIK [*sleeping, mumbling*]: Dumplings, sweet plum dumplings.

Enter PÉTER. He is twenty-one years old, also skinny as a scarecrow. His clothes are tattered and torn—the clothes of a peasant farmer. He looks over at PATRIK. He turns to address the audience.

PÉTER: He's talking in his sleep again. He does that. Pay him no mind.

PATRIK [*still sleeping*]: Oh, fresh potato bread! Too kind of you.

PÉTER: We haven't had fresh potato bread in months. Potato bread is hard to bake when you have no potatoes. We haven't had much of anything lately. No potatoes, no wheat... no rain. I remember our last rain. It was this past fall. November third, 1788. A glorious fall day. A rainbow in the sky. I tracked mud on the floor when I came in for dinner.

PATRIK [*asleep, smacking his lips*]: Such wonderful raspberry jam you have, uncle. Such a lovely red...

PÉTER: It is August now. Nine months, not a drop of rain. I tell you, it is a bad time to be a farmer in Hungary. That is what we were: farmers. Back in the east. I grew corn. Patrik raised pigs.

PATRIK [*asleep*]: Smoked sausages, my favorite!

PÉTER: There are only a few villages that have escaped the drought: river towns. The skies are dry, but the rivers teem with water, with life. [*He points to the river.*] Rivers like this. There is a town a few miles south of here, a town called Folàsz.

PATRIK [*asleep*]: Sponge cake with caramel. Uncle Bartos, you shouldn't have! I knew it... I just knew you would take us in...

PÉTER: Ah, he's having dessert. He'll be waking soon. I hope the people of Folàsz can spare us some scraps. We have walked so many miles. I do not know how many more I have left in me.

PATRIK: Delicious, uncle, delectable! [*He lets out a loud burp. It startles him awake.*] Gracious, what was that?!

PÉTER: What was what?

PATRIK: That enormous frog! I swear, Péter, it roared right in my ear.

– 169 –

PÉTER: I heard nothing.

PATRIK [*embarrassed*]: I was talking in my sleep again, wasn't I?

PÉTER: No, not at all.

PATRIK: Oh, good. I despise talking in my sleep. It is not the behavior of a gentleman.

PÉTER [*amused; they have had this conversation before*]: Patrik, my friend, we are not gentlemen. We are farmers.

PATRIK: We *were* farmers. If we expect my Uncle Bartos to take us in, we must transform ourselves into gentlemen. Uncle Bartos is a wealthy man, you know. A landowner! Very respectable.

PÉTER: I have been wondering, Patrik. How is it that you have a rich uncle in Òbuda, but the rest of your family are all laborers?

PATRIK: Are you calling me a liar?

PÉTER: Of course not.

PATRIK: Good! Because Patrik Vastag is no liar.

PÉTER: I am just curious, that is all. It is quite unusual to have a family split amongst different classes. Most times, one will find a family of laborers or a family of landowners. For a laborer to have a landowner uncle… as I said, quite unusual.

PATRIK [*proud*]: It is, isn't it? Years ago, my Uncle Bartos was a poor farmer, just like you and I. As a boy, he left for the city. He came into the service of a rich man who had no children. The man came to love my uncle as a son. When the man died, he gave his land to Uncle Bartos. Now he is a very respectable man.

PÉTER: That is a lovely story.

PATRIK: I do tell it well.

PÉTER: But you have never met this uncle, am I correct?

PATRIK: Well, I have not met him in the flesh. But I have heard of him many times. Mostly from my mother. She would always say to my father, "Ah! If only I had been smart and married your brother Bartos!" She was a funny woman, my mother. [*He clutches his stomach.*] Oh, my.

PÉTER: Are you quite all right?

PATRIK: I feel as though I have a hole where my stomach should be.

PÉTER: I have the same feeling.

PATRIK: But soon, Péter. Soon, we will reach my uncle's home. Surely, a rich man such as he is prepared for this drought.

PÉTER: Listen. Down this river there is a town called Folàsz. It is only a few miles south of here.

PATRIK: Nonsense. My uncle lives to the west. That town is out of the way!

PÉTER: Your Uncle Bartos lives five days' walk from here. We can rest in Folàsz and regain our strength for the trip.

PATRIK: I'm plenty strong now.

PÉTER: We just stopped here because you were weak from hunger.

PATRIK: I'm going to wash my face.

> [*PATRIK kneels beside the river and splashes water against his face.*]

PÉTER: Folàsz has food. The river towns always survive a drought.

PATRIK: If you don't believe that I have a rich uncle, just say so.

PÉTER: It is not that. I am just worried about you.

PATRIK: Save your worries, my young friend. I am feeling very refreshed.

PÉTER [*sniffs the air*]: Ugh, that river water… you smell like a catfish!

PATRIK: And you smell like a farmer! Come, let's continue westward. I am the one who convinced you to leave our home, and so I am the one who will bring us to food.

PÉTER: Plum dumplings.

PATRIK: Pardon me?

PÉTER: Fresh potato bread. Sweet raspberry jam, smoked sausages—your favorite! And a sponge cake with caramel.

PATRIK [*horrified*]: I *was* talking in my sleep, wasn't I? And you did not tell me! You would have let me embarrass myself.

PÉTER: Surely, your slumber-speaking will go away once you eat.

[*PATRIK scowls stubbornly at PÉTER.*]

PÉTER: I trust that your uncle will care for us when we arrive. But Uncle Bartos is far, and Folàsz is close. Come, let us take a turn southward and throw ourselves on their mercy. Surely, once they learn how far we have traveled, they will show us kindness.

PATRIK: We will see. But we are not staying. We dine, and then we continue on for my uncle's.

PÉTER [*agreeing*]: And then we continue on.

[*The two men travel off toward the town.*]

SCENE TWO

Scene: *The town square of Folàsz. Four storefronts line the back wall. The shop on the left belongs to DAVOS, age forty-two. He is a baker and seller of grains. The sign above his shop reads: "DAVOS'S BAKED DELIGHTS." The building to the right belongs to MARIA, age thirty-eight, who owns a small hotel. Her sign reads: "MISS MARIA'S BOARDING." The front door has a small window covered with a piece of wood that slides open and closed. The third storefront looks abandoned. Where the other buildings have signs, there is only a large, blank board. The fourth store, on the right end, belongs to IVAN, a fifty-three-year-old butcher. His shop and sign are the nicest. It reads: "IVAN'S MEATS AND CHEESE." In the window of the shop hang various cuts of meat, including a string of smoked sausage links on a hook.*

PATRIK and PÉTER walk slowly into town. No matter what PATRIK says otherwise, they are weak from hunger.

PATRIK: Remember, when you introduce me, I am not a farmer. I am a gentleman.

PÉTER: If you wish to pretend, I suggest you introduce yourself.

PATRIK: Such disrespect. But as a gentleman, I will not quibble.

[*PÉTER knocks on DAVOS'S door. DAVOS opens the door. He is a tall bearded man, not well-dressed, but clean.*]

DAVOS: Hello, strangers.

PÉTER: Hello, sir. My name is Péter Szántó. I am a farmer from the east.

PATRIK: And I am Patrik Vastag, a gentleman of the highest order.

DAVOS [*sniffing the air*]: Are you sure you do not mean fisherman?

– 172 –

PATRIK [*annoyed*]: And what do you call yourself, sir?

[*DAVOS points to the sign above the door. He smiles brightly.*]

DAVOS: Surely, the gentleman can read?

PÉTER: Pardon my friend, sir. Davos, is it? We are just so tired from hunger. Our land was killed by the drought. We have been traveling for days and cannot go any further. Do you have any food that you might be able to share?

DAVOS: I wish I could help, but you are not the first to travel through here. I really do not have anything that I can spare. You understand, I hope.

PÉTER: I do understand, sir. Thank you for hearing our story.

PATRIK [*cutting in*]: Are you sure that there is nothing you can spare? Not a muffin, a pastry, a slice of potato bread?

DAVOS [*thinks*]: Well, I do have something.

[*DAVOS returns inside.*]

PATRIK: You see, Péter? When a gentleman asks, he receives!

[*DAVOS comes back out with a long, sharp stick. He offers it to PATRIK.*]

PATRIK: What is the meaning of this?

DAVOS: There is a family of wild boar in the plains near here. Perhaps you can catch one with this. Good day.

[*DAVOS closes his door.*]

PATRIK: Well, this is useless.

[*He drops the stick, but PÉTER picks it up.*]

PÉTER: You never know. It may come in handy.

PATRIK: How? We don't have the speed to catch a boar. I could barely do such a thing when times were good!

PÉTER [*uses the stick for support*]: Yes, but if we do not eat soon, we'll need it to hold us up.

PATRIK: Maybe we'll have better fortune next door.

PÉTER [*reading the sign*]: "Miss Maria's Boarding."

– 173 –

PATRIK: I hope Miss Maria will show us some ladylike kindness.

> [*PÉTER knocks on the door to Miss Maria's Boarding. MARIA opens the sliding peep-window on the door and peeks out.*]

MARIA: Buzz off, ye beggars! No vacancy!

> [*MARIA slams the peep-window shut.*]

PATRIK: So much for that idea. We never should have stopped in this town.

PÉTER [*calling out*]: Please, Miss. We are not looking for boarding.

> [*MARIA opens the peep-window again.*]

MARIA: If ye don't wish to stay, what do ye want?

PÉTER: Just a pinch of your time, ma'am.

PATRIK: And a pinch of your food!

PÉTER: Well, yes. Food as well, if you can spare it. You see, ma'am, we are farmers from the east.

MARIA: Let me guess. The drought has ruined your land and so ye're forced to wander.

PATRIK: That is astounding! Do you tell fortunes?

MARIA: It is just a story I have heard many times this season. Trust me; ye're not the first to come through looking for food.

PÉTER: Can you show us some kindness, ma'am? We only need a nibble to regain our strength. Some carrots or beets—boiled cabbage, even!

PATRIK: I like mine with paprika.

PÉTER: That is not very gentlemanly, Patrik. Forgive my friend, Miss Maria.

MARIA: He's a strange one.

PÉTER: I will not argue that.

PATRIK: Hey!

PÉTER: Surely, ma'am, you have something that you can spare. You must prepare meals for your boarders, yes?

MARIA: I am sorry. I only have enough for my guests, and no more.

PATRIK: If there is any part of the meal they do not like, we would be happy to eat that.

MARIA: Are you insulting my cooking?

PATRIK: I can't insult your cooking until you let me try it!

MARIA: The nerve!

PÉTER: This is a misunderstanding. Your cooking is excellent! It must be if you have a houseful of guests. I can only imagine the wonderful smells from your kitchen.

MARIA: The smells… yes. [*She pauses.*] Now that I think about it, I do have something that will help ye. One moment.

    [*MARIA shuts the sliding peep-window.*]

PATRIK: That was a fine recovery. Good thinking, friend.

PÉTER: How about I do the talking from now on?

PATRIK: Perhaps that is for the best.

    [*MARIA opens the door to her boarding house and steps out. She is carrying a large, heavy pot.*]

PÉTER: Oh, a stew pot. Thank you, ma'am!

MARIA: It's not a stew pot, ye dunce. It's a bathing pot. Ye both stink. Especially your friend—he smells like a dead carp.

PATRIK: I smell like a catfish, madam.

MARIA: Ye may fill the pot from my well out back. But that had better be the last I hear of ye!

    [*MARIA re-enters her house and slams the door shut. PÉTER sighs heavily.*]

PÉTER: I am sorry, Patrik. I thought that the people of Folàsz would show us charity, but I was wrong.

PATRIK: It's all right, Péter. It was not a half-bad idea to come here. Besides, if I am to starve to death, I cannot think of a better person to do it with than you.

– 175 –

PÉTER: ...Thank you?

[*PATRIK knocks on the door of the third shop. No answer.*]

PATRIK: Come, this third store is empty. Let's give the butcher shop a try.

PÉTER: Maybe Ivan the butcher will feel pity. Be sure to mention that you were a pig farmer in the east.

PATRIK: I would... but I have already decided that I will be silent. I seem to offend everyone I speak to in this town. I know! I will stick to my plan, and you can tell Ivan that *you* are a pig farmer!

PÉTER: I don't like to be untruthful... but I'll try anything that will help us get some food. How do I play a pig farmer?

PATRIK: Just follow my example. You need uneven shoulders. That's because you are always leaning over to pour slop in your pigs' trough. [*PÉTER tilts one shoulder down and one shoulder up.*] You need a bent back, because pigs are low to the ground and you are always bending down to check their health. [*PÉTER bends over like a hunchback.*] And as for your face... well, all you need to do is be devilishly handsome.

[*PÉTER straightens up and smirks at his friend.*]

PATRIK: Oh, Péter, you were doing well, except for the face part.

PÉTER: Enough games. I will simply be myself. [*He knocks on the door to IVAN'S butcher shop.*] The butcher will either be kind or he will be like everyone else in this cursed town.

[*IVAN the butcher swings open his door. He is a big, muscular brute who can barely fit through the doorway. He wields a large meat cleaver in each hand.*]

IVAN: So you think you can steal from my butcher shop, do you?

PATRIK [*nervous, quiet*]: Ha-ha, wrong address! Come along, Péter.

PÉTER: Sir, we are not thieves, we are travelers in search of charity.

IVAN: A likely story. I've seen your kind before. Just last month, some "travelers" came seeking "charity." [*IVAN emphasizes the quoted words with the meat cleavers. PÉTER and PATRIK flinch noticeably each time.*] Fool that I was, I took pity. I gave them a hot meal and a nice bed of fresh hay to sleep on. Do you know what those fellows did? They snuck up on me in the night and stole away my darling Esmeralda!

PÉTER: Your wife?

IVAN: My *goose*! My beautiful pet goose. Oh, Esmeralda laid the finest eggs. They made omelets fit for a gentleman. How I loved my golden goose.

– 176 –

PÉTER: We are very sorry to hear about your goose.

IVAN: Oh, I'll bet you're sorry! Sorry that she's not here for *you* to steal. Oh, my sweet goose. My home is so quiet without her lovely honking.

PATRIK: If you can spare us a sausage, I will gladly honk for you.

IVAN: Fool, I will not fall for any more strangers' tricks. You're up to something. I can feel it in my bones. You'll not be getting any help from me. That is a promise! Now, get out of my doorway.

[*PÉTER steps forward before IVAN can close his door.*]

PÉTER: Wait, sir. If you will not help us with food, perhaps you can tell me one thing.

IVAN: What is it, you skinny bandit?

PÉTER: The shop beside yours is empty today. Do you know who owns it?

IVAN: Oh, yes. It belonged to old man Kovács, the blacksmith. Poor old Kovács… he dropped dead last winter. I suggest you do the same!

[*IVAN slams the door on PÉTER'S foot. PÉTER stumbles back, hobbling in pain.*]

PATRIK: How can we drop dead last winter?

[*PÉTER hops on one foot, using his sharp stick for balance.*]

PÉTER: My foot, Patrik, my foot!

PATRIK: Did that rotten butcher injure you?

PÉTER: I can't walk on my foot. I have to rest.

[*PÉTER sits heavily in the road. PATRIK puts his hands to his mouth.*]

PATRIK [*yelling*]: Brute! Ruffian! I'll show you!

[*PATRIK searches the ground around him. He picks up a rock the size of a potato. He winds up to toss it at the butcher shop.*]

PÉTER: Patrik! You aren't planning to throw that rock through his window, are you?

PATRIK: What else would I do with this rock? Butter it up and eat it?

– 177 –

PÉTER: Patrik, that man could rip your arms off.

[*PATRIK lowers his throwing arm, defeated. He looks at the rock.*]

PATRIK: If only we *could* eat rocks. We'd be able to feast all day. That's all we have out here. Scorched earth and rocks! Hungary would be a land of riches if rocks—

[*PÉTER begins to chuckle.*]

PATRIK [*bitterly*]: I am glad you see the humor in our fate!

[*PÉTER continues to laugh, getting louder.*]

PATRIK: What is so funny?

[*PÉTER shakes his head—he is laughing too hard to speak. He rolls backward in the dirt, clutching his stomach.*]

PATRIK: Oh, no. He's gone insane. Péter, please, gather your wits!

[*PÉTER sits up and wipes the tears of laughter from his eyes.*]

PÉTER: Oh, I have, my gentleman friend! I think I've found a way out of our situation.

[*PATRIK kneels beside PÉTER to listen.*]

PÉTER: I can't walk on this foot, so I'll need you to help me. We need to build a fire, and we need to fill that washing pot.

PATRIK [*furious*]: I don't smell that bad!

PÉTER: No, no, Patrik Vargas. We are not washing. We are cooking. If the people of Folàsz will not share food with us… well, we will just have to share some food with them!

SCENE THREE

Scene: *The town square of Folàsz, later in the day. The washing pot now rests on top of a roaring fire. PÉTER, alone on stage, holds the sharp stick beside it. There is a pile of rocks near his feet. PATRIK enters, struggling to carry a heavy bucket of water.*

PATRIK: What an odd coincidence that you hurt your foot… just before it was time to carry buckets and buckets of well water all over creation.

PÉTER: Come now, I would help if I could.

[*PATRIK huffs and puffs as he hefts the bucket along. He lifts it and dumps the water into the washing pot. It splashes—the washing pot is already mostly full.*]

PÉTER: I think that's enough water. Now, for the rocks! Drop them in nice and loudly so that all the village can hear the racket.

[*PATRIK grabs a rock and hurls it into the pot. It hits with a splash and a clang.*]

PATRIK: Hmm… that felt good! You try!

[*PÉTER picks up a rock and does the same. Clang! The men take turns hurling rock after rock.*]

PÉTER [*shouting at the top of his lungs*]: Stone soup! I can't wait to eat it!

PATRIK [*surprised*]: Goodness!

PÉTER [*whispering*]: Play along, so they'll hear.

PATRIK [*also shouting*]: There's nothing like a nice bowl of stone soup. This town has the tastiest stones I've ever seen!

[*A villager, MINYA, wanders by.*]

MINYA: What is all this racket?

PÉTER: My apologies, madam. We are making stone soup.

MINYA: Stone soup? In all my years, I've never heard of such a thing.

PATRIK: Oh, it's all the rage in the city. All the wealthy landowners eat it. We are making my Uncle Bartos's recipe.

MINYA: Landowners eat stone soup, do they?

PATRIK: Oh, certainly. Landowners can eat whatever they choose… and they choose to eat stone soup.

MINYA: How exotic!

PÉTER: Our soup is just missing a few ingredients. We already have the most important ingredient.

PATRIK: Fresh stones!

PÉTER: Without a doubt! [*PÉTER leans over the pot and smells.*] Ah, they smell terrific. But there are a few little things we need to finish this soup.

MINYA: Well… maybe I can help. If I chip in to the soup, may I have a taste?

PÉTER: Certainly! Do you have an onion? Just one. We don't want to overpower the stones, of course.

MINYA: Of course! I'll get that onion straightaway. [*MINYA heads off.*] Such nice young men…

PATRIK [*quietly*]: It's working. Your crazy plan is working!

    [*PÉTER throws another rock into the soup with a loud clang.*]

PÉTER [*hollering*]: Yum, yum. This looks like the best stone soup I've ever had!

    [*PATRIK smashes a rock into the pot. Another villager, ANDRAS, approaches.*]

ANDRAS: What is all this fuss I hear about a rock soup?

PATRIK: No, no, my good man. It is stone soup. There is a big difference.

ANDRAS: Oh, really? What is the difference?

PATRIK: Well…

PÉTER: Rock soup does not have beets in the broth. That must be why you were confused. We do not have any beets, so this probably looks like rock soup to you. Am I right?

ANDRAS: I'm not sure…

PÉTER: I don't want anyone else to be confused. Do you happen to have any beets? It would help us a great deal. If you do help, you may try the soup once it is ready!

ANDRAS: I must admit, I am curious. I think I have some beets in my hut.

PÉTER: Oh, what a relief. I really wanted to make a nice stone soup. Without beets, it would be too much like rock soup.

    [*ANDRAS hurries off.*]

PATRIK: That was close! You think very well on your foot.

    [*MINYA returns with an onion.*]

– 180 –

PÉTER [*shouting*]: Oh, I can't wait to eat this delicious soup!

MINYA [*startled*]: Does he always shout?

PATRIK: Only when we cook stone soup. How it excites him so! Is that the onion? Go ahead and put it in.

> [*MINYA drops the onion into the pot. PÉTER stirs.*]

MINYA: How long will it take?

PÉTER: Ah, stone soup is tricky. You never know how long it will take for the stones to cook all the way through.

PATRIK: You know, the stones would cook faster if we threw in some carrots.

MINYA: Would they?

PATRIK: Yes, it's the strangest thing. Do you have any carrots you could spare?

MINYA: I might!

> [*MINYA runs off. ANDRAS returns with an armful of beets. ANDRAS adds the beets to the pot.*]

PÉTER: Ah, perfect timing! These beets will really bring out the stony flavors. You should be proud. Your town has the best cooking stones I've ever seen.

ANDRAS: Why, thank you! I've never noticed.

PATRIK: He's right. Stones fit for a gentleman. Go ahead, grab a stone and throw it in!

> [*ANDRAS grabs a stone. He wipes it off on his shirt and chucks it in the pot with a clang.*]

PÉTER: Stone soup!

ANDRAS: Stone soup!

> [*DAVOS the baker tears open his door.*]

DAVOS: What is all this shouting?

PÉTER: Ah, Davos, my good man. We've decided to make a special meal: stone soup!

DAVOS [*astounded*]: Stone soup!

PATRIK: Ah, so you've heard of it! Of course you have. All the best men know of stone soup. You are free to try

– 181 –

some if you'd like.

DAVOS [*strokes his chin*]: I am rather hungry.

PATRIK: You bet your beard you are! But we had better taste the soup first.

PÉTER: We are the chefs, after all.

DAVOS: Oh, I know how you feel—I take a taste of each and every goodie I bake in my—

PÉTER: Could you lend us a spoon? Before we overcook the soup.

DAVOS: Right, right!

> [*DAVOS dashes inside and returns with a large, wooden spoon.*]

PÉTER: You are so generous. [*PÉTER takes the spoon, dips it in the pot, and slurps the hot water. He smacks his lips.*] This is a great start, but something is missing. What could it be?

PATRIK: Potatoes?

PÉTER: Yes, potatoes! Silly me. Stone soup just isn't stone soup without a hint of potato.

> [*The two men look at DAVOS.*]

DAVOS: I may have some that I can spare.

> [*DAVOS goes inside.*]

PATRIK [*to PÉTER*]: You know… this soup might actually be rather good!

ANDRAS: I am very excited to try it!

> [*DAVOS returns with potatoes. He dumps them into the pot.*]

PÉTER: Perfection! A cheer for stone soup!

PÉTER/DAVOS/PATRIK/ANDRAS [*together*]: Hooray!

> [*MARIA slides open the peep-window to her boarding house.*]

MARIA: What are ye madmen doing out here? Davos, what is this?

DAVOS: Come, Maria! We are cooking a stone soup feast!

PATRIK: And bring some paprika!

MARIA: Ye think I should give ye some paprika, eh?

PÉTER: Why, yes! Thank you for offering.

MARIA: But I didn't—

    [*MINYA returns with a bowl of chopped carrots.*]

MINYA: I have the carrots! Don't serve the soup without the carrots!

    [*MINYA dumps the carrots into the soup and stands next to PATRIK.*]

PÉTER: Ma'am, did you hear? Kind, generous Miss Maria has offered to add some paprika to the soup.

MINYA: Oh, I love paprika.

ANDRAS: It will give this stone soup some kick!

MARIA: Fine, I'll bring some out.

    [*MARIA slams the peep-window shut. MINYA sniffs the air near PATRIK.*]

MINYA: Is there catfish in this soup?

PATRIK: No.

    [*MARIA comes outside with a shaker of paprika. She begins to shake it into the pot.*]

MARIA: Just tell me how much to add.

DAVOS: This will be a fine stone soup.

ANDRAS: My stomach is beginning to grumble. [*To PÉTER.*] How about you, chef? Are you hungry?

PÉTER: You have no idea.

MARIA: Is this enough paprika?

    [*PATRIK snatches away the paprika.*]

PATRIK: Oh, no, Miss Maria, you've added too much! What were you thinking?

– 183 –

PÉTER: Too much paprika can wreck a stone soup!

ANDRAS: Even I knew that!

MARIA: I'm very sorry… ye didn't tell me when…

MINYA: Is our soup ruined?

PATRIK: Maybe not. There is one ingredient that could save this soup. And that ingredient is smoked sausage. But where, oh where, can we get a smoked sausage?

> [*ANDRAS, MINYA, DAVOS and MARIA rush toward IVAN the butcher's shop. They all begin to bang on the door. IVAN opens the door.*]

IVAN: We're closed!

DAVOS: Ivan, it is a food emergency!

MARIA: I put too much paprika in the stone soup.

ANDRAS: We need some of your smoked sausage.

> [*IVAN steps outside.*]

IVAN: Are you all fools? Can't you see that these rapscallions are tricking you? There is no such thing as stone soup.

> [*The other VILLAGERS all gasp in shock. They look over at PÉTER and PATRIK.*]

PÉTER: It's quite all right. Ivan, I forgive you.

IVAN: You forgive me?

PATRIK: I understand why you are yelling. You are just embarrassed that you have never heard of stone soup.

IVAN: Because you made it up!

PÉTER: I am flattered that you think we are so clever. But we did not invent stone soup. We only perfected it.

PATRIK: Please, do not feel bad that you have never heard of stone soup. After all, you are only a butcher.

PÉTER: And this… [*PÉTER puts an arm around PATRIK.*] *This* is a meal for ladies and gentlemen.

– 184 –

[*IVAN smirks. He glares. Then he raises his arms and smiles.*]

IVAN: Only joking! Ha-ha, of course I've heard of stone soup. My Esmeralda loved to eat it. But I must say… it really could use some smoked sausage.

PÉTER: You are a wise man, Ivan.

IVAN: All right, all right, you've twisted my arm. I'll come to your rescue.

[*IVAN goes in and pulls a line of sausage links off of a hook in his window. PÉTER and PATRIK shake hands.*]

MARIA: Hooray!

[*IVAN pulls the links apart and tosses the first one into the pot. At that moment, PATRIK lets out a loud "honk," just like a goose.*]

PATRIK: A gentleman always keeps his promises.

[*IVAN tosses more sausage links one by one into the pot. PÉTER stirs as he does.*]

PÉTER: It's almost ready! And because you saved the day, Ivan, you will get the best part!

IVAN: The best part?

PATRIK: The stones!

MARIA [*grumbling*]: Lucky.

[*PÉTER stops stirring.*]

PÉTER: All right, I think this stone soup is ready to eat. As the chef, I will take the first taste.

[*PÉTER scoops a spoonful of soup and eats it. The crowd waits anxiously.*]

PÉTER: How about that… it's good!

DAVOS: You sound surprised.

PÉTER: I mean, of course it's good! Everyone, grab a bowl!

[*PÉTER hands PATRIK the spoon. The VILLAGERS each go off and return with a bowl. PATRIK begins to ladle out servings of the stone soup. PÉTER hops forward, using the stirring stick for support. He turns to address the audience.*]

– 185 –

PÉTER: And so, our stone soup was a hit. But you'll never believe what happened next.

[*PÉTER hops back toward the empty storefront. He lifts the stirring stick and bangs it against a board. The board falls away to reveal a large sign underneath. The sign reads: "PÉTER AND PATRIK'S FINE STONE DINING." PÉTER opens the door, and each VILLAGER enters the restaurant, carrying a bowl of stone soup to eat.*]

PÉTER [*to audience*]: We never did make it out to see Uncle Bartos in Òbuda. We found that Folàsz was the perfect place for us to start a new life.

[*PATRIK lets the last VILLAGER into the restaurant.*]

PÉTER [*to audience*]: You'd be surprised at the size of our menu. It turns out that stones can be used in almost any recipe.

PATRIK: Come on, Péter! We have to finish preparing tonight's special.

PÉTER [*to audience*]: Dumplings.

PATRIK: Sweet stone dumplings!

[*PÉTER grins, then heads back into his new restaurant with PATRIK. PATRIK looks around from the doorway.*]

PATRIK: Who on earth was he talking to?

[*PATRIK shrugs and closes the door to the restaurant. End of play.*]

Two Scenes from *The Thief of Camelot*

written by Luke See
illustrated by David Rushbrook

<u>Cast</u>

KING ARTHUR	40s; powerful and respected king
QUEEN GUINEVERE	30s; admired and intelligent queen
SIR DYNADAN	20s; knight of the Round Table
SIR BRUISE	20s; a dangerous knight
VILLAGER	20s; victim of the thief of Camelot

<u>Setting</u>

The Court of Camelot. Locations around the court include the castle of Sir Bruise.

SCENE ONE

Scene: *The beautiful and shining court at Camelot. The court is set inside of a large hall. Colored flags, swords, and shields adorn the walls. The shields represent different respected knights of the Round Table. Two large thrones are placed at one end of the hall. Sitting atop them are KING ARTHUR of Camelot and his wife, QUEEN GUINEVERE. As he sits atop his throne, KING ARTHUR listens to villagers speaking. His hand rests on the hilt of a large sword that hangs at his hip. The room has a few dozen people in it, a mixture of villagers and knights in armor.*

VILLAGER [*bowing*]: Thank you, good king, for allowing me to speak.

KING ARTHUR: You are most welcome. Tell me what troubles you, villager.

VILLAGER: I believe one of your knights, a knight of the Round Table, attacked my farm.

Gasps of shock escape throughout the crowd.

KING ARTHUR [*shocked*]: Are you sure?

VILLAGER: My liege, I am quite sure of it. My only horse was stolen.

KING ARTHUR: Not simply stolen, sir! [*growing more annoyed*] You claim that it was stolen by a knight of this very court. Think hard, young man; this type of accusation is not taken lightly.

VILLAGER [*nervously*]: I mean no disrespect to you, King Arthur. [*pausing*] Perhaps I am mistaken. The last thing I desire is to lose the favor of my king. I…I…I….

GUINEVERE silently rises from her throne and walks the few short steps down toward the VILLAGER. The VILLAGER immediately drops to his knees. Whispers fill the room.

GUINEVERE [*comforting*]: Good sir, it is bad enough that you have been the victim of this crime. You certainly do not need to fear your queen. Please, rise.

Visibly shaking, the VILLAGER rises to his feet and lifts his eyes to GUINEVERE.

GUINEVERE: That's better. Now, you believe this thief to be a knight of Camelot. It is a terrible accusation, yes, but not one to be ignored. What brought you to this conclusion, sir?

VILLAGER: Thank you, Lady Guinevere, for your kind words and comfort. I am a man of simple means; my family's farm is a small cottage with a stable. Late last night, I heard a ruckus outside my window. By the time I got outside, it was too late; an armored man on horseback had seized my own horse by the reins. He rode off into the distance, pulling my poor mare along behind him.

GUINEVERE [*still kindly*]: This man you describe—although he certainly does seem to be a knight, what brought you here to Camelot? What made you think he is in the service of King Arthur?

VILLAGER: As you may recall, my lady, last night was the full moon. It lit the sky up brightly. As the knight rode away with my stolen horse behind him, I glimpsed the shield that he wore across his back. On this shield, I saw a large brown bear, a fearsome face bearing its fangs. What struck me most, though, is that the beast had one eye. This

– 188 –

is not a sigil that is easily forgotten; I knew that I had seen it before, seen it here, at the court of King Arthur. I believe it is the shield....

SIR DYNADAN [*off-stage, shouting confidently*]: ...Of Sir Bruise the Barbarian!

The crowd chatters as SIR DYNADAN enters from the far end of the hall. He is clad in shining silver armor with a white cape. KING ARTHUR stands and raises his hand, signaling for silence. The room goes quiet.

KING ARTHUR: Well met, Sir Dynadan of Camelot. Do you believe this man's tale?

SIR DYNADAN: Without question, my liege. There is no mistaking the one-eyed bear of Sir Bruise. Perhaps Sir Bruise was worthy of the Round Table once, but for many months now, he has not been seen at court. We have heard only stories of him—stories much like the one this villager has told you today. Sir Bruise is using his strength and his power to take advantage of your subjects.

KING ARTHUR [*saddened*]: It breaks my heart to hear such tidings. Sir Bruise's father was a good friend and great warrior. I knighted Bruise myself just before his father's death at the Battle of Hastings.

SIR DYNADAN: While you were away in combat, Sir Bruise began to terrorize the countryside. Many have reported their livelihoods ransacked by a knight in black armor. However, the attacks have always been under the cover of darkness. I've had my suspicions about the identity of the culprit, but with this villager's tale, we can now know for sure that Sir Bruise must be brought to justice.

GUINEVERE: Very well. Sir Bruise must be captured. Is there any loyal knight here who is up to the task?

SIR DYNADAN: Not another word, Queen Guinevere. I will seek out Sir Bruise and bring him to court so that he may answer for his crimes. He dishonors the court of Camelot—and worse, he attacks the people we are sworn to protect.

KING ARTHUR: You are a brave knight, Sir Dynadan. Camelot is lucky to have you as one of its mightiest protectors.

> *SIR DYNADAN bows and begins walking out of the hall.*

SIR DYNADAN: In no more than three days from now, I will return to this hall, riding the stolen horse of our friend here, with Sir Bruise in chains, shackled behind me!

> *The crowd erupts with cheers and applauds as SIR DYNADAN exits.*

VILLAGER [*to GUINEVERE*]: My lady, do you truly believe he might rescue my horse as well?

GUINEVERE: Sir Dynadan the Dependable always keeps his word.

> *Exit QUEEN GUINEVERE and KING ARTHUR.*

SCENE TWO

Scene: *The stable outside the castle of SIR BRUISE. The large stable's walls are black stone, and the floor is covered in hay. The stable is in a state of disorder. A few open chests are scattered about the stable, overflowing with stolen fabrics, armaments, and money. A brown horse is chained to the wall. It wears a simple saddle made of burlap. Hanging on the wall, just above a large torch, is a flag with the picture of the one-eyed bear. A large man in black armor enters the stable carrying a leather saddle.*

SIR BRUISE removes his helmet and places it on the stall door.

SIR BRUISE: Let's try this again, you foolish horse.

The second that SIR BRUISE gets near the horse, the horse releases a panicked whinny and kicks its back feet high in the air, near SIR BRUISE's face. SIR BRUISE leaps backward and slips, falling flat on his behind, the saddle thumping down on his lap. He lies flat on the stable floor and groans in pain.

SIR DYNADAN [*off-stage*]: That has got to hurt.

SIR BRUISE [*sitting up*]: Who goes there? Who dares enter my stables?

SIR DYNADAN [*off-stage*]: Your stables? Now that is interesting. I had heard your father left his castle to your elder brother, boy—not to you.

SIR BRUISE leaps to his feet.

SIR BRUISE: Do not dare to mention my father! Who goes there?

SIR DYNADAN leaps down into sight from the ceiling beams above.

SIR DYNADAN: Sir Dynadan at your service. I am a true and just knight of Camelot—unlike you, horse thief.

SIR BRUISE: You…. [*pausing*] You cannot prove anything. I am no thief! I am a nobleman of great wealth and power!

SIR DYNADAN crosses toward the brown horse.

SIR DYNADAN: Great wealth and power, you say? It is strange, then, that this mare of yours wears a simple saddle made of burlap. You have outfitted every other horse in your stable with the finest shoes and most extravagant saddles.

SIR BRUISE [*nervously*]: You don't know what you're talking about. This is my horse; I've had it for ages.

SIR DYNADAN: Truly? Is that your story? And yet this horse—whom you claim to have kept for many years—is so threatened by you that it will not even let you approach it? Excuse me, Sir Bruise, but this farce has gone on long enough. You are a thief and you know it. I am here to bring you to the justice you deserve.

SIR BRUISE draws his sword and points it at SIR DYNADAN, taking a step forward.

SIR BRUISE: You will do no such thing. Take this filthy farmer's mare and go on your way; I have no quarrel with you. Leave now, and I will not have to kill you.

SIR DYNADAN [*smiling*]: Do not worry, Bruise the Barbarian. I will return this mare to its rightful owner. But I shall do so with you as my prisoner, mounted upon this horse's rump, [*drawing his sword*] for I have given my word, in front of King Arthur of Camelot—and I am nothing if not dependable.

SIR BRUISE spits on the floor of the stable.

SIR BRUISE: I spit on the name of Arthur the Useless. If it were not for his wars and conquests, my father would be here in this stable today instead of me. I have no use for you, [*mocking*] Dynadan of Camelot. I seek only Arthur. If I must destroy you to summon him to my gates, so be it.

SIR BRUISE retrieves his helmet and puts it on. HE and SIR DYNADAN move in circles around each other. SIR BRUISE kicks up a pile of hay directly into SIR DYNADAN's face and lunges forward. Blackout.

The Olympic Games: A History of Evolving Competition

written by Vincent J. Scotto

The Olympic Games are one of the most popular sporting events in the world. More than two hundred countries competed in the 2012 Summer Olympic Games. Since the beginning, each event has featured new advances in technology. As a result, the modern Olympic Games have evolved into what some would call the most demanding athletic competitions in the world.

The modern Olympics were inspired by the original Greek Olympic Games. The original Greek Olympic Games were held in Olympia, Greece, until the fourth century CE. The modern Olympics did not begin until the late nineteenth century. The first modern Olympics were held in Athens, Greece. Now, different countries take turns hosting the Olympic Games. The hosting country needs time to prepare for all the participating athletes and audiences.

In the early days, the modern Olympic Games had fewer than fifty events. Only thirteen countries participated in the first modern Olympics in 1896. They were quite a small set of events. Only men were allowed to participate in the Games. As the world changed, though, so did the Games. For nearly thirty years, the Olympic Games struggled. The world did not seem to be interested. Many countries were wrapped up in their own problems. The first "successful" Olympic Games did not happen until 1924. Thousands of athletes competed. Female athletes could finally compete, too. From there, the Olympic Games only became more popular.

The Olympic Games have grown greatly in competition. The first modern Olympics included track and field, swimming, cycling, gymnastics, wrestling, fencing, weight lifting, tennis, and shooting. The Games were competitive for their time. Athletes are even more competitive now, though. With more than forty sports and over three hundred events, the Olympic Games are one of the largest events in international competition. The Summer Olympic Games are the most watched; however, the Games have expanded to include other major events: the Winter Olympics, the Youth Olympics, and the Special Olympics.

Richer countries have an advantage in the Olympic Games. People from richer countries have better access to training and coaching. This gives an advantage over the less fortunate. For a time, professional athletes were not allowed to participate in the Olympic Games. This was supposed to level out the talent. Professionals were eventually allowed to participate again in some sports. This made the Olympic Games much more entertaining for the public. To this day, richer countries tend to win more medals than other countries.

The Olympic Games have been a key part of international competition for more than a century. The Games have grown into what some call the most popular televised events in the world. As the world changes, so will the Olympic Games. The only thing that has not changed is the desire of athletes around the world to compete against one another.

Works Cited

"Ancient Olympic Games." *Olympic.org*, Ancient Olympics, www.olympic.org/ancient-olympic-games. Accessed 15 Feb. 2017.

Guttmann, Allen. *The Olympics: A History of the Modern Games.* University of Illinois Press, 1992.

"The Olympic Games." *History.com*, A&E Television Networks, LLC, 2010, www.history.com/topics/olympic-games. Accessed 15 Feb. 2017.

Rain Barrels

written by Mark Weimer

Most people pay for something that they could get for free: water. Buying a container for collecting rainwater costs much less than the average monthly water bill. These containers are called *rain barrels*. Everyone should have a rain barrel. Rain barrels can help ease drought, or times when there is no rainfall. They can help people save money. They can also help the environment.

It is a good idea to have some way to get fresh water. Rain barrels are a very easy way to save fresh water in areas that do not have nearby water sources. Only 3 percent of the world's water is fresh water. Billions of gallons are lost each day as rivers empty into seas. Rain barrels could help ease the difficulty of drought. Rain still falls in many areas where water is scarce. The trouble is that rainwater can often come all at once. It comes in a single heavy rain and cannot be collected and stored. Rain barrels are perfect solutions for these areas.

People who collect rainwater use it for many different purposes. They can use it to water plants and gardens or to wash their cars. Those who have city water and rain barrels will have lower water bills. They will save money each month. There is no limit to the number of barrels you can keep. If you have many barrels and regular rainfall, you can easily collect enough to have a self-sufficient home.

Homes and businesses should be required to have rain barrels. They would reduce the amount of runoff, which often hurts the environment. Increased runoff causes more erosion. Also, animal habitats are often replaced with retaining ponds. These often dry up.

When the ponds dry up, any creature dependent on the water could die.

It is a no-brainer: Everyone should have a rain barrel. Rain barrels conserve water. They help people save money. They are good for the environment. They are not hard to make, and the parts are cheap.

Charlotte's Web: A Lesson in Friendship

written by Summer York
illustrated by Walter Sattazahn

Charlotte's Web is a heartwarming story about a runt pig, Wilbur, who is saved by Fern Zuckerman, the farmer's daughter. With the help of his friend Charlotte, a smart spider who also lives in the barn, Wilbur becomes famous. Through Charlotte, Wilbur learns how to make a friend. He also learns what it means to be a good friend.

As Wilbur grows up in the barn, he has trouble making friends. One evening, a voice offers to be Wilbur's friend. It says, "I've watched you all day and I like you." Wilbur is thrilled about his newfound friend—until he meets her. She is a spider. Her looks and actions frighten Wilbur. However, after talking to Charlotte, Wilbur learns not to judge a new friend based on looks alone.

One day, Wilbur discovers that he is in danger of becoming Christmas dinner. He is terrified until Charlotte creates a plan to save his life. She plans to spin words about Wilbur into her webs, including "Some Pig," "Terrific," "Radiant," and "Humble." Charlotte's webs make Wilbur so famous that his life is no longer in danger. By spinning her webs, Charlotte shows Wilbur that she is willing to give time and hard work to help her friend.

Toward the end of the story, Wilbur asks Charlotte why she helped him. She replies, "By helping you, perhaps I was trying to lift up my life a little." In saying this, Charlotte teaches Wilbur that helping a friend also "lifts up" the one who helps. In other words, a friendship helps both friends. This teaches Wilbur the true meaning of friendship.

Charlotte's friendship teaches Wilbur three important lessons about friendship. He learns that friends can be different, friends help each other, and friendship is good for both friends. Thus, Wilbur cherishes Charlotte's friendship for the rest of his life.

Works Cited

White, E. B. *Charlotte's Web*. Harper & Brothers, 1952.

Presentation Nerves

written by Summer York
illustrated by Matthew Casper

Daniel sat in social studies class and tapped his pencil on his workbook. Learning about the United States was so boring. *Who cares what the capital of Alaska is?* Daniel thought to himself. He kept glancing at the clock, wishing that class would just end already. After social studies was gym class, and Daniel could not wait to get outside for dodgeball.

"All right, class," Miss Bruno said to get everyone's attention, "since you're all doing so well with state capitals, we're going to start working on our next project. I want each of you to pick a U.S. state and research interesting facts about it. Then, you will give a five-minute oral presentation to the class about what you learned." Everyone in the class groaned and rolled their eyes.

Oh, no! Daniel thought in a panic. He had never given an oral presentation before. He didn't want to have to speak in front of the entire class. What if he forgot what to say or started sneezing in the middle of his speech? Everyone would laugh at him. His stomach flip-flopped just thinking about it. In fact, he wasn't even excited to play dodgeball anymore. He felt miserable for the rest of the day.

After school, Daniel told his grandfather about the social studies assignment. "Well, kiddo," his grandfather said, "just picture everyone in their underwear!" His grandfather chuckled and went back to reading the newspaper. Daniel was not sure how that could help him. His grandfather just didn't get it sometimes. Daniel went to find his older sister. Dena was in sixth grade, so she had probably spoken in front of her class before.

"Oh, I can't stand oral presentations," Dena complained, sipping a soda. "I always get super nervous before I have to do that. One time, this kid in my science class was giving an oral presentation, and he threw up right in the middle of it! I hope that doesn't happen to you!" Dena laughed as she grabbed her soda and headed for her room.

"You're not helping!" Daniel yelled. He went to his own room. Now he was more nervous than ever, even though the presentation wasn't until next week. After he finished his homework, he decided to start researching his state. He had been assigned Alaska, of course, because that had to be the most boring state. He found a few articles online, but he could not focus on reading them. Every time he thought about speaking in front of the class, his palms started to sweat.

"Daniel, you didn't eat much," his mom said after dinner. "Are you feeling all right?" She placed a cool palm on his forehead. Daniel told her about his oral presentation and how nervous he was about it.

"Honey, everyone gets nervous about speaking in front of people," she told him. "I'm sure that all of your classmates are just as nervous as you are."

"But what if I throw up?" Daniel asked. His mom shook her head, remembering how Dena had told that story over and over when it happened in her science class.

"You won't throw up," she insisted. "You'll write your speech, and then you'll practice it until you know

it well. Then, on the day of the presentation, remember that everyone is nervous. You'll have to be supportive of your classmates. You should listen to their speeches and clap when they finish so they know they did a good job. Then, they'll do the same for you."

Daniel thought about what his mom said. She usually gave good advice. Maybe all of the students were feeling the same way he was right now.

"I'll bet that once you give your presentation," his mom continued, "you'll see that it wasn't as bad as you thought." She smiled, opened the freezer, and got out the ice cream for dessert. Ice cream always made Daniel feel better.

The following week, it was time for the social studies presentations. Daniel held his notecards in his jittery hands and tried to remember what his mom had said. Everyone looked pretty nervous. Each time a presentation ended, though, Daniel's stomach felt like it was doing cartwheels.

"Daniel, are you ready?" Miss Bruno finally asked. He nodded and slowly stood. For a few seconds, he had a flash of terror and wanted to run out the door. But he was sure they would find him eventually—there was nowhere to hide. Instead, he took a deep breath, walked to the front of the room, and began.

"Alaska is the 49th state. It became a state on January 3, 1959. There are many interesting facts about Alaska." After a few sentences, Daniel started to relax, and the five minutes flew by. When he finished and everyone clapped, he felt relieved. He had actually learned a lot, and he didn't throw up after all.

The Value of Timed Writing Exercises

written by Jennifer Tkocs

You sit at your desk, computer in front of you. To your side is a timer set for 15 minutes. All distractions are gone. The television is off. Your phone is set to silent mode. For the next quarter of an hour, it's just you, your keyboard, and a writing prompt.

Does this sound intimidating? It may if you are unfamiliar with timed writing exercises. However, timed writing exercises can be beneficial. They can improve your skills as a writer.

What is a timed writing exercise? A timed writing exercise describes a stretch of time in which you focus only on writing. Often, you can set the time limit for yourself. For example, you may choose to write for 10 minutes or 15. Your goal is to shut off distractions and focus entirely on the words during that time. It is helpful to have a prompt to guide what you write.

One benefit of a timed writing exercise is the lack of distractions. It can often be hard to focus when you begin to write. You steal glances at the television. You chat with your family members. You worry about chores you did not complete. By removing all distractions for a set amount of time, you can focus on the writing itself and not the things going on around you.

Setting a time limit can help you be better organized. You can get to the core of one or two points without having to deal with the rest of the details. You may have a chance to flesh out details in a later, longer writing session. However, the short session forces you to stay on topic and get right to the point. If you are working on several sections for a longer piece of writing, you can use several short timed writing exercises to work on each part.

Finally, timed writing exercises force you to focus on crafting new material rather than editing. Many writers feel that their "inner editor" gets in the way of creating new stories. A timed writing exercise forces you to push the editor away and focus only on moving forward in your scene, story, or essay.

Apple

written by Summer York

The first bite is a waxy, crispy crunch, the red skin tasting bitter and chewy. The burst of juice makes my taste buds leap, twirl, and dance. Round and round I crunch, enjoying the mix of tart skin and pleasant flesh. When the skin is gone, my teeth sink deeply into the soft white insides—tangy and sweet all at once. The succulent crisp tastes of harvest conjure scenes of orchards, hayfields, and cozy autumn comforts. The core leaves my fingers with a sticky sweetness as I eat every last bit of delicious apple goodness.

Turning Off Niagara Falls: A New Report

written by Summer York

June 12, 1969

This is Channel 5 News' Al Smith, reporting live from Niagara Falls. The gushing water of the Niagara River spilling over the American Falls has altogether stopped. Currently, the waterfall is a dry cliff. A spectacular and dangerous project is underway.

Today, the U.S. Army Corps of Engineers has finished building a dam to block the flow of water over the American Falls. This marks the beginning of a six-month-long project. Hopefully, it will save one of America's most beautiful natural wonders.

The project began after geologists raised concerns about erosion. They feared that erosion would cause the waterfall to collapse. Niagara Falls flows at a constant rate exceeding 4.5 million gallons of water per minute. That flow has been steadily eroding rocks at the top of the falls. As a result, boulders as big as houses have been crashing to the riverbed below. Geologists warned that such erosion might eventually cause the American Falls to disappear.

The dam is in place, and the water has been diverted to Horseshoe Falls. Army Corps scientists will now conduct studies on the dry cliff and riverbed. Their goal is to determine the true threat of erosion. They will also make repairs to the rock face. Workers will even drop over the edge of the falls to fix problems with the vertical ledge.

This is the first undertaking to block the flow of the Niagara River over the falls. Howard Mills, a spokesman for the Army Corps of Engineers, called the project necessary. "Something like this has never been attempted," he said earlier today, "but we felt that we had to take on the task. An iconic landform is at risk."

Such a breathtaking display has drawn record crowds. Thousands of people came to watch workers finish the dam. Visitors were permitted to walk on the dry riverbed, which has never been done before. Extra police officers were called in to manage the massive crowds.

The Channel 5 News team has been talking to visitors throughout the day. The reactions have been the same. Everyone we spoke to has been awed by this once-in-a-lifetime happening.

"I never thought I would see anything like this," said Marvin Horowitz of Cleveland, Ohio. "What an amazing sight!" Horowitz brought his wife and four children to Niagara Falls. They had been planning the trip for quite some time.

Alice Stevenson is a resident of Buffalo, New York. She heard about this project and planned a day trip to the falls. She said, "My husband and I brought our two children, my sister, her husband, their kids, and my parents. We felt it was important for everyone to see something that few people will ever get to see firsthand."

All of Niagara Falls' attractions will be open to the public during the work. The Visitor Center is open seven days a week year-round. Channel 5 News will continue to provide updates about this ongoing project.

Works Cited

MacClennan, Paul. "Man Stills Niagara's Thunder, and Falls Remain Spectacular." *The Buffalo News*, 12 June 1969, p. A1.

Madrigal, Alexis C. "What Niagara Falls Looks Like without Water." *The Atlantic*, 12 Jan. 2014, www.theatlantic.com/national/archive/2014/01/what-niagara-falls-looks-like-without-water/282991/. Accessed 15 Feb. 2017.

"Niagara Falls History Questions." *NY Falls*, nyfalls.com/niagara-falls/faq2/. Accessed 15 Feb. 2017.